EXPLORING
·SCIENCE AND·
MEDICAL
DISCOVERIES

Reproductive Technology

Other books in the Exploring Science and Medical Discoveries series:

EXPLORING

SCIENCE AND
MEDICAL
DISCOVERIES

Reproductive Technology

Clay Farris Naff, Book Editor

GREENHAVEN PRESS
An imprint of Thomson Gale, a part of The Thomson Corporation

THOMSON
━━━✦━━━ ™
GALE

Detroit • New York • San Francisco • San Diego • New Haven, Conn.
Waterville, Maine • London • Munich

THOMSON
GALE

Bonnie Szumski, *Publisher*
Helen Cothran, *Managing Editor*

© 2006 Thomson Gale, a part of The Thomson Corporation.

Thomson and Star Logo are trademarks and Gale and Greenhaven Press are registered trademarks used herein under license.

For more information, contact:
Greenhaven Press
27500 Drake Rd.
Farmington Hills, MI 48331-3535
Or you can visit our Internet site at http://www.gale.com

Cover photograph reproduced by permission of © Nogues Alain/CORBIS Sygma.

LIBRARY OF CONGRESS CATALOGING-IN-PUBLICATION DATA

Reproductive technology / Clay Farris Naff, book editor.
    p. cm. -- (Exploring science and medical discoveries)
    Includes bibliographical references and index.
    ISBN 0-7377-2833-7 (lib. : alk. paper)
    1. Reproductive technology. 2. Human reproductive technology.
    3. Human reproductive technology--Case studies. I. Naff, Clay Farris.
    II. Series.
    RG133.5.R469 2006
    616.6'9206--dc22
                                                        2005054269

Printed in the United States of America
10 9 8 7 6 5 4 3 2 1

Contents

Chapter 2: Modern Reproductive Technologies

Chapter 3: Personal Experiences with Reproductive Technology

Chapter 4: Contemporary Controversies over Reproductive Technologies

Foreword

Most great science and medical discoveries emerge slowly from the work of generations of scientists. In their laboratories, far removed from the public eye, scientists seek cures for human diseases, explore more efficient methods to feed the world's hungry, and develop technologies to improve quality of life. A scientist, trained in the scientific method, may spend his or her entire career doggedly pursuing a goal such as a cure for cancer or the invention of a new drug. In the pursuit of these goals, most scientists are single-minded, rarely thinking about the moral and ethical issues that might arise once their new ideas come into the public view. Indeed, it could be argued that scientific inquiry requires just that type of objectivity.

Moral and ethical assessments of scientific discoveries are quite often made by the unscientific—the public—sometimes for good, sometimes for ill. When a discovery is unveiled to society, intense scrutiny often ensues. The media report on it, politicians debate how it should be regulated, ethicists analyze its impact on society, authors vilify or glorify it, and the public struggles to determine whether the new development is friend or foe. Even without fully understanding the discovery or its potential impact, the public will often demand that further inquiry be stopped. Despite such negative reactions, however, scientists rarely quit their pursuits; they merely find ways around the roadblocks.

Embryonic stem cell research, for example, illustrates this tension between science and public response. Scientists engage in embryonic stem cell research in an effort to treat diseases such as Parkinson's and diabetes that are the result of cellular dysfunction. Embryonic stem cells can be derived from early-stage embryos, or blastocysts, and coaxed to form any kind of human cell or tissue. These can then be used to replace damaged or diseased tissues in those suffering from intractable diseases. Many researchers believe that the use of embryonic stem cells to treat human diseases promises to be one of the most important advancements in medicine.

However, embryonic stem cell experiments are highly controversial in the public sphere. At the center of the tumult is the fact that in order to create embryonic stem cell lines, human embryos must be destroyed. Blastocysts often come from fertilized eggs that are left over from fertility treatments. Critics argue that since blastocysts have the capacity to grow into human beings, they should be granted the full range of rights given to all humans, including the right not to be experimented on. These analysts contend, therefore, that destroying embryos is unethical. This argument received attention in the highest office of the United States. President George W. Bush agreed with the critics, and in August 2001 he announced that scientists using federal funds to conduct embryonic stem cell research would be restricted to using existing cell lines. He argued that limiting research to existing lines would prevent any new blastocysts from being destroyed for research.

Scientists have criticized Bush's decision, saying that restricting research to existing cell lines severely limits the number and types of experiments that can be conducted. Despite this considerable roadblock, however, scientists quickly set to work trying to figure out a way to continue their valuable research. Unsurprisingly, as the regulatory environment in the United States becomes restrictive, advancements occur elsewhere. A good example concerns the latest development in the field. On February 12, 2004, professor Hwang Yoon-Young of Hanyang University in Seoul, South Korea, announced that he was the first to clone a human embryo and then extract embryonic stem cells from it. Hwang's research means that scientists may no longer need to use blastocysts to perform stem cell research. Scientists around the world extol the achievement as a major step in treating human diseases.

The debate surrounding embryonic stem cell research illustrates the moral and ethical pressure that the public brings to bear on the scientific community. However, while nonexperts often criticize scientists for not considering the potential negative impact of their work, ironically the public's reaction against such discoveries can produce harmful results as well. For example, although the outcry against embryonic stem cell research in the United States has resulted in fewer embryos being destroyed, those with Parkinson's, such as actor Michael J. Fox, have argued that prohibiting the development of new stem cell lines ultimately will prevent a timely cure for the disease that is killing Fox and thousands of others.

Greenhaven Press's Exploring Science and Medical Discoveries series explores the public uproar that often follows the disclosure of scientific advances in fields such as stem cell research. Each anthology traces the history of one major scientific or medical discovery, investigates society's reaction to the breakthrough, and explores potential new applications and avenues of research. Primary sources provide readers with eyewitness accounts of crucial moments in the discovery process, and secondary sources offer historical perspectives on the scientific achievement and society's reaction to it. Volumes also contain useful research tools, including an introductory essay providing important context, and an annotated table of contents enabling students to quickly locate selections of interest. A thorough index helps readers locate content easily, a detailed chronology helps students trace the history of the discovery, and an extensive bibliography guides readers interested in pursuing further research.

Greenhaven Press's Exploring Science and Medical Discoveries series provides readers with inspiring accounts of how generations of scientists made the world's great discoveries possible and investigates the tremendous impact those innovations have had on the world.

Introduction

People throughout history have gone to extraordinary lengths to overcome infertility. In ancient Egypt, physicians would insert garlic into the vagina to diagnose infertility. If the woman awoke the next morning with a taste of garlic in her mouth, she was healthy. If not, doctors thought it likely that she had blocked fallopian tubes. Unfortunately, women whose tubes were obstructed—a common cause of female infertility—had to resort to amulets and ritual journeys to fertility shrines for a cure. Fertility shrines were hardly unique to ancient Egypt. They also appeared in cultures as diverse as the Celtic and the Japanese. Nor are fertility pilgrimages confined to the past. Even in modern times, thousands of infertile people have sought a miraculous cure from the waters of the Catholic shrine at Lourdes, in France.

More recently, though, science has begun to offer technological solutions to infertility. As far back as the late nineteenth century, artificial insemination with donated sperm has enabled infertile couples to conceive. However, only since 1978 have assisted reproductive technologies—known as ART—become a major phenomenon in American life. In that year the first "test-tube baby" was born through a process known as in vitro fertilization (IVF). Gynecologist Patrick Steptoe and biomedical researcher Robert Edwards pioneered the IVF techniques needed to fertilize a human egg in a dish and then implant it in a woman's womb to allow for normal development and delivery. Since then, the U.S. market for ART reached $6.5 billion in 2004 and is expected to reach $10 billion by 2009. Even so, consumer popularity does not indicate universal acceptance. Indeed, reproductive technologies face persistent opposition, and as the technology develops, opposition will certainly increase.

Condemnation of IVF

Until recently, the lightning rod for much of the opposition to reproductive technologies has been IVF. Some conservative religious authorities regard it as an impermissible intervention in natural procreation. The Catholic Church has been firm in its rejection of IVF. Its reasons are spelled out in a 1987 Vatican document called *Donum Vitae*. According to the document,

> The conjugal act by which the couple mutually expresses their self-gift at the same time expresses openness to the gift of life. It is an act that is inseparably corporal and spiritual. It is in their bodies and through their bodies that the spouses consummate their marriage and are able to become father and mother. . . . Fertilization achieved outside the bodies of the couple remains by this very fact deprived of the meanings and the values which are expressed in the language of the body and in the union of human persons.[1]

Some other religious leaders join the Catholic hierarchy in objecting to the practice in IVF, which involves the creation of multiple embryos, only some of which will be implanted. A standard procedure in IVF is to fertilize several eggs at once, then pick out several of the most promising candidates for full-term pregnancy. The remaining ones may be stored in deep freeze or simply discarded. In many instances multiple embryos are implanted and then some are aborted as they develop, a procedure known as selective reduction. Many religious leaders believe that this destruction of embryos constitutes the taking of human life.

The Connection Between IVF and Stem Cell Research

The IVF issue has been complicated by the rise of another biomedical technology that draws on IVF. Stem cell researchers use embryos stored in fertility clinics to obtain the embryonic stem cells that are generated in the earliest stages of development, when the embryo is known as a blastocyst. These cells can become any tissue in the human body, and scientists hope that they can be used to repair tissues and cells damaged as a result of disease or injury.

However, the rise of stem cell research has greatly increased religious opposition to any procedure that involves the destruction of embryos, including IVF. In May 2005 President George W. Bush publicly praised a faith-based group, the Snowflakes Frozen Embryo Adoption Program. The group has worked on behalf of unwanted IVF embryos by encouraging couples to "adopt" them through implantation and bring them to term rather than let scientists use them for research. Surrounded by some of the children born from such adoptions, Bush remarked, "I believe America must pursue the tremendous possibilities of science, and I believe we can do so while still fostering and encouraging respect for human life in all its stages. . . . The children here today are reminders that every human life is a precious gift of matchless value."[2]

Support from Liberal Theologians

Not all religious denominations or leaders oppose IVF or stem cell research. Religious supporters of such technologies note that none of the major Western religions traditionally recognized conception as the moment of a personhood. In a June 2005 letter to senate majority leader Bill Frist in support of stem cell research using embryos created during IVF, more than forty religious leaders representing various Christian, Islamic, and Jewish congregations wrote,

> As theologians and clergy, we are very aware of the debate regarding the moral status of the embryo. Perhaps the greatest contribution of the Abrahamic religions—Judaism, Christianity and Islam—is the core conviction that each and every person is a unique creation of infinite value. . . . We are also aware that faith traditions disagree over when a human

being becomes ensouled. . . . We believe that as a nation, it is far better to pursue a path where there is common moral ground. One place of agreement is the shared belief among major religions that we have an obligation to relieve suffering and heal the sick. . . . Couples who no longer need . . . embryos for reproductive purposes should be allowed to donate them for research and treatment of disease, to relieve suffering and promote healing.[3]

Nevertheless, religious opposition to IVF may be gaining the upper hand in America. One reason is that opposition to other kinds of biomedical research has focused new attention on the destruction of embryos associated with IVF. In July 2005 the Associated Press reported a growing consensus against IVF:

An Illinois judge declares an early embryo is a human being, allowing a couple to sue a clinic for destroying a fertilized egg. A U.S. senator suggests couples seeking fertility treatment should not be allowed to produce more embryos than they wish to implant simultaneously. Anti-abortion activists picket a fertility clinic in Virginia, proclaiming, "IVF kills babies." These and other developments have some reproductive health experts wondering if opposition to embryonic stem cell research may broaden to include in vitro fertilization, a mainstream medical procedure used by millions of people.[4]

Distinguishing Babies from Embryos

Secular ethicists take a different view of the status of embryos, claiming that they are not equal to human beings. Amnon Goldworth, senior medical ethicist at the Packard Children's Hospital in California, observes,

Personhood is a social construct that is shaped not only by an understanding of objective nature but also by community needs and values. . . . These needs and values find their expression in the way we see things. . . . However, many do not "see" a human countenance in the pre-embryo. For them, personhood is conferred on human organisms with whom human interactions are possible or occur. We can cuddle a baby; we cannot cuddle a zygote. We coo at an infant and he or she responds by smiling; zygotes do not smile. An infant grasps a proffered finger; a zygote cannot. Babies have personalities and embryos do not. That is why babies are persons and embryos are not.[5]

Secular attempts to determine precisely when personhood should be conferred on a developing human have not resulted in consensus. There is, however, a nearly unanimous view among secular bioethicists that embryos in the earliest stages of development—those used in IVF, stem cell research, and other controversial procedures—are not persons. The *Boston Globe* summed up this viewpoint in a 2005 editorial: "The embryos in question, called blastocysts, are microscopic organisms consisting of fewer than 200 cells. They are less than two weeks old, and most of them the unneeded products of in-vitro fertilization procedures. These clumps of cells do not have a moral claim to personhood."[6]

Feminist Opponents of IVF

Although the debate over the status of the embryo is at the center of the IVF controversy, some of those opposed to reproductive technologies are not concerned about embryos but about women. Self-proclaimed "radical" or "social justice" feminists have condemned reproductive technologies. Many of these critics argue that ART, rather than increasing women's reproductive choices, dehumanize women. Feminist scholars Joan C. Callahan and Dorothy E. Roberts offer their key objection to IVF: "Since reproduction-assisting technologies contribute to a system of social subordination . . . they are harmful." They add:

Policies governing procreation not only affect individual interests; they also shape the way we value the members of social groups. Trading genetic material and women's reproductive capacity on the market misvalues women's reproductive labor, exalts the importance of genetic relatedness, and devalues the genetic contribution of people of color. It therefore reinforces gender, class, and racial inequality.[7]

Feminist author and professor Janice Raymond goes further in her denunciation of reproductive technologies. In her book *Women as Wombs*, Raymond argues that IVF and similar technologies reduce women to empty vessels waiting to be filled with babies for the benefit of men. Feminist opponents have formed an international organization to ban ART and related technologies. The loose-knit group is called the Feminist International Network of Resistance to Reproductive and Genetic Engineering (FINRRAGE). Its influence has been felt primarily in Europe, where opposition to genetic engineering of any kind (including genetically modified foods) is much stronger. Notwithstanding this fact, according to a 2002 report by the European Society of Human Reproduction and Embryology, the number of IVF attempts in western Europe, at 250,000 a year, is more than double those in the United States.

Human Reproductive Cloning

If IVF and the production of excess embryos have raised controversy, the specter of human reproductive cloning has generated almost unanimous opposition. In reproductive cloning an offspring is born with precisely the same DNA as another currently or previously existing animal. The technology involves a process called "somatic cell nuclear transfer" (SCNT). During this procedure, scientists extract genetic material from the nucleus of an ordinary (somatic) adult cell—as opposed to a gamete, or germ-line cell, such as a sperm or egg. The nuclear DNA is then inserted into the center of a hollowed-out egg. The egg is then jolted with electricity to make it fuse and start dividing into an embryo. From that point on the process is much like IVF. Once the cloned embryo has become a blastocyst, it is implanted into the womb of a host female, where it develops until birth.

The first successful instance of reproductive cloning in mammals through SCNT occurred in 1997, when Ian Wilmut and his colleagues at the Roslin Institute in Scotland produced Dolly the sheep. Advances in mammalian cloning have come swiftly since then, and human embryos have been cloned for research purposes, but no credible claim of human reproductive cloning has yet been made. (The Raelian sect announced it had cloned a human baby but failed to deliver proof. Similar claims by others have also lacked any documentation.)

Nevertheless, strenuous objections to the idea of reproductive cloning have been voiced around the world. Religious concerns about the moral status of the embryo have been amplified in the debate over cloning. Another worry is that clones would be treated poorly by society because of the repulsion felt by most people when contemplating human cloning. Many conservative theologians also regard the technology as a violation of God's design, which intends for babies to be born to two parents out of a loving sexual union. The strongest opposition has come from the Catholic Church, which calls human cloning intrinsically evil. Evangelical Christians have been nearly as adamant in their opposition. There has been a generally negative response from Jewish and Islamic religious leaders to the idea of human reproductive cloning as well. One Saudi cleric called for the death penalty for cloning. The position of Eastern religions, such as Hinduism and Buddhism, seems to be more tolerant of the idea of human cloning.

To be sure, opposition to human reproductive cloning is much broader than is opposition to any other reproductive technology. A 2002 poll of Americans found that 77 percent opposed human reproductive cloning. Even those directly involved in the fertility treatment industry tend to oppose reproductive cloning, at least for the present, largely on grounds of safety: Many clones are born with birth defects or genetic syndromes that appear later in life and doom them to an early death.

The European Society of Human Reproduction and Embryology issued a statement in 2001 reiterating its support for a ban on reproductive cloning. In it, the society, which represents fertility practitioners in Europe, stated, "We strongly oppose the recent proposal to attempt human reproductive cloning. While we fully acknowledge the distress that infertility can cause, the available assisted-reproduction techniques can provide very successful treatment for the vast majority of infertile couples."[8]

Similarly, in the United States a panel convened by the National Academy of Sciences and related organizations to study the implications of human cloning concluded in 2002 that a ban on reproductive cloning should remain in place for at least five years. The panel left the door open for a possible change of policy in the future:

> The scientific and medical considerations related to this ban should be reviewed within 5 years. The ban should be reconsidered only if at least two conditions are met: (1) a new scientific and medical review indicates that the procedures are likely to be safe and effective and (2) a broad national dialogue on the societal, religious, and ethical issues suggests that a reconsideration of the ban is warranted.[9]

In 2003 an international network of science academies also called for a continued worldwide ban on reproductive cloning. However, reflecting the secular consensus on the distinction between persons and embryos, all of these scientific societies endorsed a continuation of therapeutic cloning, which involves the production of embryos for research purposes. These are never implanted in wombs.

Making Cloning a Crime

Unlike IVF, human cloning faces legal bans with criminal penalties in many countries. Great Britain enacted such a ban in 2001, although it permits therapeutic cloning. Some forty-six other countries, including nations as diverse as Mexico, Germany, Israel, India, and Japan, have also passed legislation outlawing human reproductive cloning. In the United States administrative prohibitions have been in place while Congress considers legislation to criminalize cloning. Even the United Nations is considering a global ban on human cloning.

What this trend suggests is that as ART develops along different fronts, opposition to its use will likely intensify. Indeed, the growing promise of reproductive technologies brings with it increasingly difficult ethical conundrums. For some people, religious principles dictate opposition to such technologies. For others, libertarian principles require that consumers be allowed to choose what is best for them. Many others endorse some of the procedures but not others. The debate over reproductive technologies will continue to play out in the courts, the media, legislative bodies, religious institutions, scientific academies, and businesses as society tries to reach some consensus on how to balance freedom of choice with the protection of human life.

Notes

1. Congregation for the Doctrine of the Faith, "*Donum Vitae:* Instruction on Respect for Human Life in Its Origin and on the Dignity of Procreation," February 22, 1987. www.priestsforlife.org/magisterium/donumvitae.htm#11.
2. George W. Bush, "President Discusses Embryo Adoption and Ethical Stem Cell Research," May 24, 2005. www.whitehouse.gov/news/releases/2005/05/200505 2412.html.
3. James Forbes Jr. et al., "Letter from Clergy Regarding Stem Cell Research," Coalition for the Advancement of Medical Research, June 2005. www.camradvocacy.org/fastaction/news.asp?id=1496.
4. Associated Press, "Battle over Embryos Opens New Front: In Vitro Fertilization," July 11, 2005. www.beliefnet.com/story/170/story_17059_1.html#cont.
5. Amnon Goldworth, "The Ethics of In Vitro Fertilization," *Pediatrics in Review,* August 1999, p. 38.

6. *Boston Globe,* "Stem Cell Imperative," January 23, 2005. www.camradvocacy.org/fastaction/news.asp?id=1264.
7. Joan C. Callahan and Dorothy E. Roberts, "A Feminist Social Justice Approach to Reproduction-Assisting Technologies: A Case Study on the Limits of Liberal Theory." www.uky.edu@buddy/FeministSocialJusticeApproach.htm.
8. European Society of Human Reproduction and Embryology, "Statement from the European Society of Human Reproduction and Embryology," March 15, 2001. www.grg.org/HouseClone.htm.
9. Committee on Science, Engineering, and Public Policy, *Scientific and Medical Aspects of Human Reproductive Cloning.* Washington, DC: National Academies Press, 2002, p. 99. www.nap.edu/openbook/0309076374/html/99.html.

CHAPTER 1

The Rise of Reproductive Technologies

Artificial Insemination and Animals

R.H. Foote

The development of artificial insemination (AI) began more than a century before the first recorded attempts to try the procedure with humans. The knowledge gained in working with animals eventually made it possible to artificially inseminate women. In the following selection veterinary researcher R.H. Foote reviews the history of animal artificial insemination. The first documented instance, involving an artificially inseminated dog that gave birth to three pups, took place in 1784, he reports. However, rigorous research into AI techniques did not get under way until 1899, when E.I. Ivanow began to try insemination techniques in various livestock, pets, and other animals. Following the efforts of the pioneering Russian, intensive research and development took off in numerous countries. Later in the twentieth century, researchers invented ways to dilute and preserve bull sperm, making it possible to fertilize many cows from one prize source. Antibiotics were added to clear the sperm of venereal diseases. In 1949 a technique to freeze and later revive bull sperm was invented, and freezing methods continued to be improved over the next several decades. The next major breakthrough, in the 1980s, was the sorting of sperm into male and female. By the end of the twentieth century, the use of artificial insemination had laid the groundwork for other reproductive technologies, including cloning. R.H. Foote is a professor emeritus of reproductive physiology at Cornell University.

Artificial insemination (AI), as practiced by bees and many other flying insects, has played an important role in plant reproduction for a very long time. Use of AI in animals is a

R.H. Foote, "The History of Artificial Insemination," *Journal of Animal Science*, vol. 80, 2002, pp. 1–8. Copyright © 2002 by the American Society of Animal Science. All rights reserved. Reproduced by permission. Edited from the original for clarity and length.

human invention and more recent. Undocumented tales exist of Arabs obtaining sperm from mated mares belonging to rival groups and using the sperm to inseminate their own mares.

However, our story starts with recorded history, where facts are available to document noteworthy achievements. Consequently, the story is related chronologically. Much of the development of AI occurred before the 1980s when electronic networks became available, so earlier references are included. The developments that made AI the most important animal biotechnology applied to date include improved methods of male management and semen collection, evaluation, preservation, and insemination. Detection of estrus and control of the estrous cycle in the female also were important. The development of AI is a remarkable story of tireless workers dedicated to the pursuit of knowledge, to the replacement of fiction with facts, and the application thereof.

Dairy cattle will be emphasized because AI has had the greatest genetic impact in that species. Other species overviewed include swine, horses, sheep, goats, dogs, rabbits, poultry, and endangered species. . . .

Early History of AI

[Microscope developer Anton] Leeuwenhoek (1678) and his assistant, Hamm, were the first persons to see sperm, which they called "animalcules." Leeuwenhoek did not have an advanced formal education, so he did not study Latin, the scientific language of the day. However, he was a clever, capable individual who ground lenses so precisely (one still exists today with 270 magnifications) that sperm were visible. His published paper amazed, and perhaps amused, the reigning king of England, who regularly read papers submitted to the Royal Society, where Leeuwenhoek's paper was published.

Another century passed before the first successful insemination was performed by [Italian scientist Lazzaro] Spallanzani (1784) in a dog, which whelped three pups 62 [days] later. Spallanzani originally trained to be a priest, but he had a great interest in natural history and pursued the latter. He was a professor of natural history in Pavia by the age of 25. He collected, analyzed, and classified a large array of butterflies, shells, and other marine and land animals. His abode was overrun with many collections, somewhat to the consternation of relatives living there. But he used these for rigorous, comparative objective analysis to discern much about animal physiology and characteristics of fitness.

Another 100 [years] passed before [British biologist Walter] Heape (1897) and others in several countries reported that AI had been used in isolated studies with rabbits, dogs, and horses. Heape was an outstanding reproductive biologist, establishing much of the basis for the relationship between seasonality and reproduction. This led to Cambridge becoming a world center for reproductive studies.

Russian Research

Pioneering efforts to establish AI as a practical procedure were begun in Russia in 1899 by [E.I.] Ivanow. By 1907 Ivanow (also transliterated as Ivanov or Ivanoff) had studied AI in domestic farm animals, dogs, foxes, rabbits, and poultry. Some of this research, especially in horses, is included in a paper in English submitted June 21, 1922, and published in record time in the July 1922 issue of the *Journal of Agricultural Science.* He developed semen extenders and trained technicians to select superior stallions and multiply their progeny through AI. Much of the AI work in Russia was taken over later by [V.K.] Milovanov (1938), described in a text translated into English. He established major projects for sheep and cattle breeding. He did not E-mail his orders for supplies. In his own workshop, Milovanov designed and made practical artificial vaginas and other items, many similar to those used today. This was an enormous improvement over the earlier method of collecting semen from sponges placed in the vagina of mount animals. . . .

News of the extensive use of AI in Russia following the Ivanoff (1922) report became widespread in the Western world with the publication of the book on AI by [Arthur] Walton (1933). Walton conducted a number of experiments, including a pioneering shipment of ram semen to Poland, which 2 [days] later was used for successful insemination of ewes. However, commercial AI did not evolve rapidly in the United Kingdom.

Some AI work, particularly with horses, had been performed in the early 1900s in Denmark. Eduard Sørensen, at The Royal Veterinary College in Copenhagen, Denmark, was familiar with the Russian work. With [Jacob] Gylling-Holm, Sørensen organized the first cooperative dairy AI organization in Denmark in 1936. The program enrolled 1,070 cows the 1st [year] and 59% conceived, slightly better than natural service in the same herds. This was an important stimulus for the development of AI in dairy cattle in the United States and other Western countries.

The Danish veterinarians established the method of rectovaginal fixation of the cervix, allowing semen to be deposited deeply into the cervix or into the body of the uterus. This technique provided a tremendous advantage because fewer sperm were required for insemination of each cow. Another Danish "invention" was the straw for packaging semen. In 1956 I saw some of the original oat straws that Dr. Sørensen kept in his desk. Subsequently he saw children at a birthday party for his daughter sipping punch with cellophane straws, and he recognized that he had found the straw that he needed. . . .

Meanwhile, the much earlier research by Spallanzani led eventually in Italy to the development of an artificial vagina for dogs by [Giuseppe] Amantea in 1914. This work served as a model for the Russian development of artificial vaginas for bulls, stallions, and rams. Another Italian [Telestor] Bonadonna, continued research on AI in several species. His enthusiasm for the potential value of AI, along with [Nils] Lagerlöf, resulted in the establishment of the highly successful International Congress on AI and Animal Reproduction held every 4 [years].

In Sweden, Lagerlöf became known for his research on infertility problems in bulls. This research was stimulated by his visit with W.W. Williams, a Cornell D.V.M. [Doctor of Veterinary Medicine] who had published methods of staining spermatozoa. . . .

Phenomenal growth of AI occurred in the 1940s in the United States. The procedures developed in the United States became established worldwide. In 1936, [R.L.] Brownell was inseminating cows in the Cornell herd, and other AI work was started in the late 1930s in Minnesota and Wisconsin. In 1938, an AI cooperative was established in New Jersey, modeled after the Danish system. Another one in 1938 followed in the state of New York. The development of the New York Artificial Breeders, Cooperative, Inc., currently Genex, Inc., in Ithaca, New York made possible the close collaboration between a farmer cooperative and researchers and extension personnel at Cornell University. This was a highly productive relationship resulting in the experimental insemination of hundreds of thousands of cows and publication of more than 100 research papers on sire selection, testicular evaluation, semen collection, evaluation and processing; and fertility testing. . . .

Semen Evaluation

The most widely used test of sperm quality from the initial stages of AI development until the present time has been the assessment of the proportion of normal, progressively moving sperm. Thus, a good microscope is the key. In addition to examining sperm with brightfield microscopes, differential interference contrast microscopes, multiple stains, flow cytometry, and computer-assisted sperm analysis (CASA) have contributed to improved quantification of sperm motion. With frozen semen, evaluation of post-thaw survival became important. . . .

Ejaculate volume and sperm concentration are the two other critical components of semen evaluation because they determine the number of sperm obtained. Volume originally was measured in graduated containers. . . .

Fertility of sperm is the ultimate test of sperm quality. Often it is not possible to measure fertility, so many tests of semen quality in addition to motility and morphology, such as the hypoosmotic swelling test, mucous or gel penetration, and integrity of the DNA have been correlated with fertility. Competitive fertilization with mixed sperm offers an efficient way to rank the fertility of males either using in vitro fertilization tests or tests with animal insemination. However, it is not generally feasible to mix semen in commercial AI. For commercial AI, an inexpensive method of estimating fertility, based on cows not returning for insemination, was developed as an essential component of the AI program. This made possible the comparing of fertility of bulls, inseminators, semen processing procedures, and even herd performance under practical field conditions. It provided a remarkable new system of recording breeding efficiency. Others had argued strongly for using pregnancy diagnosis, but this clearly involved few cows, was performed sporadically, and did not provide for centralized collection and evaluation of data. The efficiency of the nonreturn method for monitoring fertility is reduced today because of multiple suppliers of semen to individual farms and within-herd inseminators.

Innovations Extend Life

Initially the most important problem to resolve was a method to store semen long enough for shipment and use in the field. The first major improvement in the AI procedure initiated in the United States was the development of a yolk-phosphate semen extender. [G.W.] Salisbury et al. (1941) improved the media by buffering the egg yolk with sodium citrate. Sperm survival at 5°C permitted use of the semen for up to 3 [days] and the citrate dispersed the fat globules in egg yolk, making sperm visible for microscopic examination. This semen extender was used worldwide for cattle. Glycerol was added later for cryopreservation of bull sperm.

The next major stimulus to AI of dairy cattle was an improvement of about 15% in fertility resulting from a better method of initially protecting sperm from cold shock and the control of some venereal diseases by the addition of antibiotics. The Cornell extender, containing the antibiotic mixture of penicillin, streptomycin, and polymyxim B, was used for many years as the standard. Many years were required to eradicate the diseases from bulls. During that time in vitro treatment of semen with antibiotics prevented transmission of several diseases. Antibiotics are still included as "insurance" protection against possible contamination. This treatment of semen was worth hundreds of millions of dollars to the dairy world. No patents were filed, and neither Pennsylvania nor Cornell received any remuneration. The reward was service to agriculture. Growth of AI was now ensured, because dairies using only AI eliminated venereal diseases, reduced embryonic death, and achieved high fertility.

With AI expanding rapidly, demands for semen from popular bulls increased. The simplest way to meet this demand was to "stretch" each ejaculate farther by using fewer sperm per insemination, providing that this could be accomplished without sacrificing fertility. Salisbury and coworkers published several classic papers clearly supporting the concept that only a few million sperm per insemination were required. In conducting these experiments Salisbury was criticized by some who declared that "dilution" of semen was like "watering the milk." Consequently [R.H.] Foote and [R.W.] Bratton (1950) introduced the word "extender" because the yolk-citrate-antibiotic medium enhanced and extended the usefulness of semen. This word has "stuck." We considered using the word "suspender" as a snappy term, also. The net result of these experiments was that semen extension could be increased at least 25-fold. . . .

Selection of Bulls for Milk

One of the major reasons for initiating AI was to make the males that transmit superior genetics for milk production available to more producers in the animal industry. This was democracy in action. The elite bulls would not be limited to the wealthy. However, bull selection procedures practiced before the AI era gave disappointing results. Many bulls with high proofs in natural service did not repeat in AI. . . .

While the geneticists were making breakthroughs on sire selection, an astounding achievement was reported from England, the successful freezing of chicken sperm by including glycerol. Glycerol soon was found to be useful for bull sperm. Many researchers had tried to freeze bull semen (I had even tried ethylene glycerol unsuccessfully in the late 1940s to store bull sperm at $-10°C$) but had failed. A bit of serendipity played a role in the discovery. The research had focused on using sugars as cryoprotectants, but they did not lead to successful results. However, [researcher Christopher] Polge relates that he returned 6 [months] later to try again, and results were promising, presumably with the same bottle of fructose stock solution. Why success now? What was in the bottle? Chemical analysis showed that the bottle contained no sugar, but rather glycerol and protein in proportions comprising Meyers albumin used for histology. Apparently, there had been a mistake in labeling when reagents were stored. . . .

Methods of Freezing

Packaging frozen semen for use with solid carbon dioxide (Dry Ice®) or liquid nitrogen was a problem. Glass ampules often broke during freezing or thawing. [R.] Cassou (1964) modified the system developed by Sørensen (1940), with a method for sealing plastic straws and a gun for insemination. Originally 0.5-mL capacity straws were used, but 0.25-mL straws are popular because they require less storage space.

Another major change in storage occurred in the 1950s with the shift from solid carbon dioxide storage at −79°C to liquid nitrogen at −196°C. Researchers had demonstrated that sperm survival at −196°C was virtually infinite, whereas biologic changes occurred with storage at −79°C. Also, storage with solid carbon dioxide was not convenient, and frequent resupply was necessary.

Liquid nitrogen storage also was a problem, because insulation of the tanks was inefficient. Frequent refilling was required to maintain a safe temperature of about −196°C. Manufacturers of tanks were not interested in improving tanks until J. Rockefeller Prentice, owner of American Breeders Service, privately provided a substantial sum of money, which convinced Linde Division of the American Cyanamid Company that there was a market for liquid nitrogen containers with improved insulation. The successful cryopreservation of sperm and development of efficient liquid nitrogen containers provided the foundation upon which today's entire cryopreservation industry is built.

Frozen semen is less fertile than fresh semen, as many semen additives to improve fertility of frozen semen have been tested with minimal success. However, a recent report provided preliminary support for a peptide that increased fertility when added to frozen-thawed semen. . . .

One of the most dramatic technical advances in recent years is the sexing of sperm by DNA quantification using flow cytometry instrumentation developed at Livermore Laboratories and improved since. The time currently required to sort the billions of sperm per ejaculate limits extensive commercial application, but the machines are getting faster. . . .

Knowledge Gained

In the initial stages of attempting to develop AI there were several obstacles. The general public was against research that had anything to do with sex. Associated with this was the fear that AI would lead to abnormalities. Finally, it was difficult to secure funds to support research because influential cattle breeders opposed AI, believing that this would destroy their bull market. The careful field-tested research that accompanied AI soon proved to the agricultural community that the technology applied appropriately could identify superior production bulls free from lethal genes, would control venereal diseases, and did result in healthy calves. Thus, fear was overcome with positive facts. The extension service played an important role in distributing these facts.

The knowledge gained from the AI experience was extremely helpful in stepwise development of each successive reproductive technology, such as frozen semen, superovulation, embryo transfer, and, eventually, cloning. Simultaneously, the public became better informed and more willing to accept that technology developed with worthy goals, and built-in ethical application, could produce positive change, benefiting the whole community. Worthy goals, development of the necessary knowledge and skills, and ethical considerations all are essential components of any technology that will result in a positive impact on society and the environment. Thus, the impact of AI was much more profound than simply another way to impregnate females.

Eugenics and the Rise of American Sperm Banks

Cynthia R. Daniels and Janet Golden

As the following selection explains, the practice of obtaining sperm from anonymous donors and using it for artificial insemination (AI) has a long history in the United States. The authors, political scientist Cynthia R. Daniels and historian Janet Golden, assert that from the beginning eugenics—the idea that offspring can be improved by selective breeding—has played a guiding role in the development of AI. Beginning in 1884, donors were selected based on physical appearance. In the first half of the twentieth century, when eugenics gained widespread legitimacy, other traits—including some noninheritable characteristics, such as membership in a particular religion—were selected as well, the authors note. Despite a growing repugnance for eugenics following World War II, the authors argue, eugenic ideas shaped the practices of the new sperm banks being established in America. Prospective parents believed they could have better babies through the careful selection of sperm donors. With the development of techniques to freeze sperm, marketing gurus at sperm banks are able to collect and preserve sperm from famous donors and use the lure of eugenics to attract customers seeking the ideal baby. Cynthia R. Daniels is an associate professor of political science at Rutgers University in Camden, New Jersey. Janet Golden is associate professor of history at Rutgers.

A contemporary visitor to one of the largest sperm banks in the United States would find a dazzling array of seminal products available for purchase. The storage room of New England Cryogenics—in "home run" distance from Boston's

Cynthia R. Daniels and Janet Golden, "Procreative Compounds: Popular Eugenics, Artificial Insemination, and the Rise of the American Sperm Banking Industry," *Journal of Social History*, vol. 38, Fall 2004, pp. 1–10. Copyright © 2004 by the *Journal of Social History*. Reproduced by permission.

Fenway Park—contains more than 165,000 vials of sperm representing the best that American men have to offer. Consumers can peruse donor catalogs listing the race, ethnicity, height, weight, hair color, hair texture, skin tone, facial structure, IQ hobbies, talents, and interests of the men whose sperm is for sale. The semen that is selected can then be purchased for about $165.00 per "straw" with additional charges for shipping and handling. In the U.S., tens of thousands of children are conceived each year through artificial insemination with semen purchased from sperm banks.

Both sperm donors and their "donations" are subjected to stringent forms of testing and screening to insure not only their health, but also the marketability of the product they produce. At most sperm banks, donors may be rejected if they are too young (under 21) or too old (over 35); if they are too short (under 5'8") or too tall (over 6'2"); if they weigh too little or too much. They may be rejected if they are adopted or have parents who are adopted because of an inability to obtain a complete genetic and family history. Other reasons for exclusion include having had sex with another male, with a woman who has had sex with a bisexual male, or with more than a maximum number of sexual partners. A family history of as many of one hundred different diseases or physical disorders can likewise rule out potential donors. Once accepted as a donor, a man can be rejected if he fails one of the monthly blood and urine tests administered to check for drug use, HIV, and a range of other infectious diseases. As one newspaper article noted "being accepted as a sperm donor can be as difficult as entering Harvard." The data suggest otherwise. It is easier to get into Harvard.

Once past the battery of tests, donors are numbered and categorized by race and ethnic origin. Donors at the largest and most successful sperm bank in the world, California Cryobank, are "hand printed." A biometric identification device records a three-dimensional measurement of the donor's hand which is used to confirm the identity of the donor for future visits, or as Cryobank puts it, "to ensure that the man standing at the donor desk really is donor #500." Samples in vials are then both numbered and color-coded by racial categories: predictably, white caps for Caucasian; black for African-American; yellow for Asian, red for "all others." Sperm banks then sell the seminal product through catalogs which feature glossy photos of virile men. In short, in contemporary society, sperm is a commodity, alienated from its producer and yet sold as the embodiment of that producer's particular traits. . . .

This article traces the role of populist eugenics in shaping artificial insemination with donor sperm (AID) from doctor-dominated AID practiced from the 1920s through the 1960s through the rise of the modern cryobanking industry which supported a consumer-dominated AID in the late twentieth century. It begins by examining the development of AID and the eugenic interests it provoked and then turns to the rise of the modern sperm bank, exploring the growth of the industry and the ways in which it markets the "traits" of donors, playing to popular notions of heritability that have no scientific standing. Scholars have discussed eugenics as a social movement resting on the unproven scientific claim that, by controlling the breeding of those deemed unfit or genetically defective and encouraging the breeding of the fit, the quality of the population could be improved. . . .

Strangers as Sperm Donors

In the United States, artificial insemination developed along two tracks. One involved the treatment of female infertility in married women through the placement of her husband's sperm into her cervix—a procedure today referred to as "artificial insemination by homologous" (by husband) or AIH. The other track used donated sperm for the treatment of male infertility, or artificial insemination by donor (AID). AIH occurred first and, although controversial because it violated standards of female modesty, was nonetheless reported in the medical literature. J. Marion Sims described experiments in uterine insemination in the 1860s, including his repeated inseminations of six women. Only one case resulted in a pregnancy which was later miscarried. The treatments were typically instituted because the patients suffered from malformed cervixes which blocked the entry of sperm into the uterus.

AID developed in response to male infertility. First used in 1884, it was not described in the medical literature until twenty-five years later, and by an observer rather than the physician who undertook the procedure. Addison Davis Hart, whom historian Elaine Tyler May believes was the sperm donor, wrote that Philadelphia physician William Pancoast administered donated semen to a wealthy, anesthetized Quaker woman who had been under his care for the treatment of infertility. Upon discovering the husband to be azoospermic (having no spermatozoa in the semen) Pancoast arranged for the wife to be chloroformed under the pretext of undergoing a minor surgery and he then inseminated her with the sperm of the allegedly "best looking member" of his medical class. The insemination proved successful and the woman was never told how she became pregnant. Hart's reference to the fact that the doctor chose the best looking donor suggests that even at an early date, AID was seen as offering an opportunity to create a better baby. The fact that the insemination was kept secret suggests that practitioners were reluctant to tread upon the shaky moral and legal grounds on which such a procedure rested.

Prior to the 1930s few cases of AID were reported in the medical literature. Duluth, Minnesota, physician, R.T. Seashore, reported finding only twenty-four articles in the American medical literature. He provided the twenty-fifth when he reported his own case. In this instance, a couple married for six years became parents with his assistance, which included drawing up legal papers and finding a donor as well as performing the procedure. "To all appearances," he noted "they are a happy father and mother and betray no evidence of regret on their part," a statement that perhaps indicates something of the uncertainty physicians felt about the practice. Other physicians writing about AID in the 1930s focused their discussion on the most effective techniques—including the collection of semen, the nutrient medium in which it was to be maintained, and the choice of equipment to be used when injecting it into the patient—and on the legal issues involved in the procedure.

Physicians implicitly argued that AID was a therapeutic option that had to be carefully controlled. Doctors had to use astute judgment in determining who required treatment and, of those needing help, which families could endure the strain inevitably produced by AID. They also had to be willing to engage in a morally suspect and legally questionable act. Sperm was procured by choosing an appropriate donor and asking for a masturbation sample for pay. When doctors placed the semen in the recipient they took the risk of creating a pregnancy outside of marriage. Secrecy thus benefited the physician, the woman receiving the sperm, any child born as a result of the procedure (who were called "artificial bastards" by some critics) and the husband whose infertility needed to be masked from public view. By choosing a donor whose physical characteristics resembled those of the husband, the needed secrecy could be maintained. At least one practitioner used sperm from the blood relative of the husband; most others preferred donors unknown to the couple in order to avoid emotional complications.

Matching Donor Characteristics

The commonplace assumption that children resembled their parents became, in the hands of early practitioners of AID, a mandate to match not only the physical but the social characteristics of sperm donors with the men they would make into fathers. Popular beliefs that "racial" identity involved both physical characteristics and personality infused the practice of AID with a pseudoscientific mandate. New York physician and eugenics advocate Frances I. Seymour tried to match husbands and donors by temperament and background so that a "phlegmatic German" would not be bringing up a "quick, fiery-tempered Italian youngster." Another physician, following the policies of Seymour and her colleague Alfred Koerner, chose donors between 30 and 35 and of proven fertility, arguing for careful matching lest parents "who are both sandy-haired Scots" be embarrassed by presenting "to the world a dark-eyed Spanish brunette." . . .

Accounts of AID in the popular press suggest that in the midst of the Great Depression with marriage rates falling, birth rates in steep decline, couples seeking effective techniques of birth control and growing numbers of women seeking illegal abortions, Americans began to contemplate openly new ways of overcoming infertility. Magazine articles about AID helped to normalize what some viewed as an immoral medical act, promoting acceptance of those resorting to AID and of those born as a result of its use. Woven into these reports were periodic discussions of the eugenic benefits of AID. In 1938, *Time* magazine profiled a sperm donation center established at Georgetown University School of Medicine. Its founder, physician Ivy Albert Pelzman, was described as carefully assessing the heredity and background of his donors—a list of fifteen men drawn "mostly from medical students and interns who are glad to get the $25 fee per insemination." Pelzman, like his peers, was pleased when AID succeeded and when, thanks to successful matching, the child had the appropriate physical characteristics. He proudly reported that in one instance a Chicago woman who bore two children conceived with AID heard from her friends that they "look just like their father." The article concluded with a description of the donor list that mentioned Pelzman offered sperm not only from blondes, brunettes and redheads, but also Jews, Catholics and Protestants. Physical traits such as hair color were heritable; religion was not. The fact that Pelzman bowed to his clients' interest in matching donor and husband by religion suggested that the public and the press, as well as medical professionals, understood inheritance more broadly than scientists would define it. Having been taught about better breeding in school classrooms, at county fairs and in popular writings, Americans looked to practice it when they were forced to depend on new reproductive technologies in order to become parents. Later, scientific advances would help nurture the eugenic possibilities of AID, as the practice came to be seen not only as a way of responding to male infertility but as offering a means of preventing medical problems. As an article in *Collier's* entitled "Born to Order" explained, artificial insemination would not just be employed by "free-thinking, scientific-minded intellectuals" but by "conservative, solid citizens" and for medical reasons, such as Rh [blood type] incompatibility.

Genetic Screening

The development of screening tests to identify carriers of particular traits or fetuses with particular inherited conditions was a singular achievement in twentieth-century medicine. Sheldon Reed, a geneticist who coined the term "genetic counseling" in 1947 characterized his work in medical genetics as "a kind of genetic social work without eugenic connotations." But in relieving individual suffering, the practices of medical geneticists would contribute profoundly to the idea that human beings could control the quality of the children they produced and indeed, some of the earliest proponents of medical genetic screening advocated its use for "biological race betterment." Even where medical genetics was not understood by its practitioners as supporting a eugenics program, its development clearly spurred popular imagination. Families turning to AID understood that they were making a reproductive choice that offered the potential to create better babies through the careful selection of sperm donors.

Popular literature contributed to this perception. A *Literary Digest* article, summarizing the medical and legal arguments of Seymour and Koerner and titled "Eugenic Babies," described how they too rejected professional donors as semen salesmen and relied instead on educated middle-aged men of good health and family history and "an interest in genetics." A more jocular tone and a more skeptical approach to eugenics came in the *American Mercury* article described earlier in which the author considered whether "Lucy Stoners" might want to use AID to bypass "Dame Nature." Referring explicitly to the work of Seymour and Koerner, the author asked, perhaps facetiously, whether the wife who hesitated to "bear and heir for a lord and master whose I.Q. is low may choose to conceive by implantation from Genius Vial 70703-B, double strength." Despite the humor aimed at the less than perfect husband, the author employed the language of eugenics elsewhere in the article discussing how "it would be difficult to imagine a greater medical error than to allow a couple of dark-skinned Mediterraneans to become the ostensible parents of a Nordic blood." The terms "Nordic" and "Mediterranean" were favored racial categories of eugenicists and of those who supported immigration restriction and feared the "mongrelization" of the races. Obviously, it was the job of the physician to make sure such "mongrelization" did not occur.

As the medical and popular literature of the 1950s and 1960s made clear, consumer expectations helped shape medical practice and clinical findings even as physicians retained control over reproductive technologies. Families no longer accepted barrenness as an "act of God" and increasingly sought medical intervention when it occurred. An article in *Time* magazine reported there were "at least 10,000 test-tube children in the U.S. (some doctors estimate as many as 40,000)" and by 1960 *Newsweek* offered the figure 50,000 or more.

However, as AID became more common and with the magazines calling the children born from AID "the most loved children" growing attention had to be paid to the unresolved legal and religious questions raised by the practice.

Until laws conferred paternity upon the husband and kept the wife from being charged with adultery in cases of divorce or in requests for child support, physicians sometimes sought to obtain signed approval from all parties involved before undertaking AID. The author of an article in a 1940s medical journal reported conferring with the Bureau of Legal Medicine at the American Medical Association (AMA) and their determination that AID was not illegal because it had not been prohibited by law. The Bureau also suggested that the husband of the woman receiving the insemination undertake adoption proceedings for any child born to her. The finding was widely repeated in the medical literature. Religious rulings could not of course be issued by the AMA. The popular press followed the controversy in England after the Archbishop of Canterbury appointed a commission to examine artificial insemination and ruled that the procedure was acceptable when the husband was the donor but not when conception evolved from "extramarital donorship" because it would be a breach of marriage. The press also reported the ruling of the Catholic Church that techniques that helped the husband's semen move from the vagina into the uterus were acceptable, but AID and AIH that involved the collection of sperm via masturbation was not.

Despite legal questions and religious objections, AID became a popularly accepted if religiously contested treatment for infertility by the middle of the twentieth century. Controlled by individual physicians who selected donors and determined which couples might be eligible for such intervention, the practice of matching the physical and social characteristics of donors was firmly in place to both disguise the child's paternity and the husband's sterility and, where possible, to produce "superior" offspring. The unstated medical guidelines of AID incorporated both a scientific understanding of heritable traits and a kind of hoped for positive populist eugenics, and both remained critical elements as the practice moved from physician to consumer control and as new techniques for preserving semen began to be developed.

Sperm on Ice

As new technologies led to the substitution of fresh donor sperm with vials of frozen sperm, the collaboration of physicians and patients broke down. The power to select donors increasingly rested not with the paternalistic physician but with the consumer who handed over the credit card to pay for the product. However, populist eugenics remained a powerful force in this transaction, as it had been in the private inseminations conducted decades earlier. Purchasers continued to select semen according to non-heritable traits of the donors (as well as heritable ones) and, playing to this interest, sperm banks sold their product by advertising the characteristics of donors. What consumers wanted to buy was more than a means of remedying nature's unfairness, they wanted to buy what they perceived to be the best that nature and science could, together, provide.

Populist eugenics drove consumers; scientific interest in eugenics propelled those who managed the technology. At a roundtable conference on the integrity of frozen spermatozoa held at the National Academy of Sciences in Washington, D.C., in 1976, J.K. Sherman discussed briefly the benefits of germinal choice with benefits extending beyond the infertile couple to "fertile couples wishing to improve upon the genetic constitution of their offspring." The term for this practice was "eutelegenesis" a word coined in 1935 by Herbert Brewer writing in *Eugenics Review.*

Donor insemination would not reach its full medical or market potential until the development of techniques that allowed human sperm to be frozen and then thawed and used. Cryopreservation of sperm came in to use in the cattle industry during the 1950s (producing, by 1972, more than 100 million calves from frozen bull sperm). During the 1930s, 40s, and 50s scientists had experimented with various methods of preserving human sperm through freezing, including the use of dry ice and liquid nitrogen. But human sperm proved more fragile than that of bulls, often losing its ability to impregnate an egg in the cold storage process. The problem was unsolved until 1953 when two reproductive physicians, reported the births of four children conceived with frozen semen. With the safety of frozen human sperm assured, the opportunity to create human sperm banks arose, although questions remained about the safety of the practice, whether pregnancy rates were the same for fresh and frozen sperm, and whether freezing damaged the genetic material.

Like their predecessors, some reproductive and genetic scientists involved with sperm banking perceived the tremendous potential of the technology for purposes of "positive eugenics." In 1965, Nobel prize–winning geneticist Hermann Muller, who viewed traditional eugenics as reactionary and flawed, promoted the use of frozen sperm as one element of what he termed "parental choice." Techniques of donor insemination, he argued, could be used to "rationalize" human reproduction. He explained that "the means exist right now of achieving a much greater, speedier, and more significant genetic improvement of the population. . . ." The obstacles to such improvement, he asserted, "were purely psychological ones, based on antiquated traditions from which we can emancipate ourselves. . . ." Muller advocated the establishment of banks "of stored spermatozoa . . . derived from persons of very diverse types, but including as far as possible those whose lives have given evidence of outstanding gifts of mind, merits of disposition and character, and physical fitness." With the specter of nuclear destruction haunting the postwar world, Muller, who discovered that radiation caused heritable changes in reproductive cells, proposed the creation of a "seminal Fort Knox" to store the semen of men about to be exposed to radiation. From there, the next step would be "completely planned fatherhood," as a means of avoiding paternity by those with a "dubious genetic endowment." In addition to worrying about the unleashing of the atom, Muller feared that modern medicine was keeping alive the "bearers of defective genes."

Many in the field of reproductive medicine shared his hopes and fears as well as his fascination with the eugenic potential of sperm banking. A 1966 article in *Science Digest* quoted University of Michigan physician S.J. Behrman, Director of the Center for Research in Reproductive Biology regarding the potential of frozen sperm. "The day when we can preserve the sperm, the life cells, of an Einstein or a Beethoven for reproduction in future centuries is a long way off. Someday it should be possible to identify the chromosomes responsible for certain characteristics and produce a child with exactly the characteristics desired." Behrman, a pioneer in the field of cryopreservation, favorably quoted Muller and advocated the use of cryopreservation for purposes of positive eugenics in a lecture delivered at the Annual Meeting of the American Association of Obstetricians and Gynecologists. As one listening physician affirmed in response, "We need shed no tear over the lost lineage of the azoospermic husband," one presumably rendered infertile by processes of "natural selection." The human race would replace aristocratic lineage and hereditary monarchy with the new lineage of positive genetic planning—planning guided by "thoughtful scientists and clinicians" willing to develop semen freezing to the full extent of its potential.

Banking on Nobel Laureates

Indeed, there was talk of creating a sperm bank for geniuses.

And the fantasy soon turned to reality. A promoter of popular eugenics, millionaire entrepreneur Robert Clark Graham, created a sperm bank for Nobel Laureates and other designated men of genius—the Repository for Germinal Choice—in 1976. Interestingly, the highly controversial organization met with lukewarm support from C.O. Carter of the Eugenics Society in London, who found fault with the scientific theory underlying this concept. Most offspring, he pointed out, would regress to the mean of the highly selected donor and the presumed "more moderate intelligence of the mother." The same point—regression to the mean—was acknowledged by one of the donors, Nobel Prize winner William Shockley, who had been disappointed in his own children who had regressed to the mean because their mother lacked his intellectual endowment. Nevertheless, supporters and clients of sperm banks held out hope that at the very least, the children born as a result of AID would resemble those who lived in the fictional town of Lake Wobegon where all the children were above average. Early popular accounts of children born through AID had made just such a claim.

Despite the enthusiasm of sperm banking progenitors, most medical practitioners continued to use fresh semen for artificial inseminations during the 1960s and early 1970s. Thawed semen still produced lower rates of conception and the general public viewed the practice with suspicion, despite claims that children conceived using frozen sperm were not only healthy, but of superior "stock" to those conceived naturally or, more precisely, that they had fewer birth defects. By 1977, decades after the opening of the first sperm bank only 1,000 had reportedly been born from frozen sperm. A 1978 article in the American Fertility Society's journal, *Fertility and Sterility*, noted that "the early enthusiasm for using frozen semen has been tempered. . . . The ideal method for freezing gametes has not yet been found, and the commercialization of sperm banking has not developed. . . ."

Nevertheless, reproductive scientists continued to work on alternative methods of freezing and thawing sperm in order to improve rates of conception and make frozen sperm more competitive with fresh. In the mid-1970s reproductive physicians developed a "cryofreezer"—an "easy-to-operate, precise, spermfreezing instrument" which could freeze "pellets" of sperm in a mere 20 minutes. By the end of the decade, techniques had been developed to successfully cool semen with liquid nitrogen down to a temperature of -196 degrees centigrade. In medical journals, leaders in the field of cryopreservation declared: "Thawed semen produces babies" and that "instances of conception occurring from semen preserved longer than 10 years have been recorded." In addition, they argued, "the safety of thawed semen for clinical insemination exceeds that of fresh semen. The literature indicates that abnormal spermatozoa are killed by the freezing-thawing process. Thus, only the fit and healthy sperm survive." As a result, they argued, there were lower rates of spontaneous abortion (less than 8 percent, compared to the norm of 10–15 percent) and dramatically lower rates of birth defects (less than 1 percent, compared to the norm of 6 percent) when frozen sperm was substituted for fresh sperm from the father. Nature no longer trumped science.

Although sperm banks demonstrated their scientific usefulness, their commercial potential was slow to be recognized. In 1976, Joseph Feldschuh, medical director of IDANT, the world's largest sperm bank, lamented that the enterprise, which once had six branches in different cities, had lost money and reduced its services. Eventually, the value of sperm banks began to be acknowledged in the medical community and with continuing public demand for AID, the bottom line for commercial efforts improved. Sperm banks arose to store indefinitely thousands of specimens in a single location. Customers grew to include men wishing to deposit "insurance sperm" before undergoing chemotherapy or vasectomies or before going off to war. Then, after the discovery of HIV/AIDS, freezing came to be seen as providing greater safety to consumers, because it allowed for testing for infectious disease both at the time of deposit and six months later. Additionally, frozen sperm offered purchasers access to the same donor for repeated inseminations. And, significantly, frozen sperm banks allowed purchasers, whether couples or single women, to order products from men possessing particular characteristics. Decisions about what kind of sperm to buy meshed personal concerns, populist eugenic beliefs and scientific findings that together constructed the quest for a better baby than nature could create. . . .

Marketing the Image of Success

To a significant degree, the selling of sperm was like the selling of any other commercially marketed product; advertised goods were swathed in imagery that promised what could not be bought. In this regard, the convertible sold with reference to the sex appeal of the driver, the beer marketed as a way to have a good time with members of the opposite sex, the clothing that promised to attract a good-looking partner, and the sperm hawked as having come from a Harvard man, were similar. However, while few consumers may have believed that dressing right or owning the swiftest vehicle would deliver what the advertisements promised, the eugenic message of sperm banks was transmitted to buyers who may not have understood (or wanted to know) that human beings were more than the sum of their genetic parts and that many valued characteristics—such as religious background—were not genetically determined.

In 1969, there were ten sperm banks in the U.S. Twenty years later, the number had grown to 135. Nevertheless, many physicians persisted in using "fresh sperm"—a product that had become increasingly dangerous. A Congressional Office of Technology Assessment report in 1988 found that about 11,000 physicians were practicing artificial insemination on their patients, with most physicians buying fresh donor sperm from medical students, residents and other physicians. Their continued reliance on fresh sperm resulted in a reported six cases of HIV infection in the United States between 1986 and 1989. By the mid 1990's, physicians in Canada and Australia had also reported HIV cases from donated fresh sperm. In the wake of this news and with growing concerns about the worldwide AIDS pandemic, demand for cryopreserved sperm—sperm that could be held "on ice" until donors tested clean for HIV as well as other infectious diseases—increased.

Concerns about HIV combined with the development of relatively simple equipment for sperm freezing and storage in liquid nitrogen tanks to make sperm banking a growth industry. However, while sperm banking services grew, the industry remained unregulated and unorganized. . . .

Oral history interviews with leading sperm bank directors indicated that the industry underwent a process of increasing corporate concentration from 1995 to 2001. The expense of recruiting donors and screening them for HIV and hereditary diseases raised the costs of business and drove small operators, such as individual physicians' offices, out of the market. The contraction in the number of suppliers and the growth in the size of the remaining sperm banks reshaped the industry. By 2001, only 28 sperm banks (defined as facilities which collect, store and offer sperm for sale) were operating in the U.S., based on information collected from the Sperm Bank Directory, the American Association of Tissue Banks, the Association for Reproductive Medicine, and the Food and Drug Administration (FDA). The 28 banks were located in 16 different states, but most highly concentrated on the east and west coasts and in the upper mid-west. All shipped specimens nationally, with some requiring shipment to physicians only and others shipping to private individuals (for home insemination) as well. Only one sperm bank was non-profit (the Sperm

Bank of California, founded in 1982 as an offshoot of the Oakland Feminist Women's Health Center). Three sperm banks, all in California, explicitly stated that they served non-traditional families and lesbian couples. A fourth bank, Hereditary Choice in California, specialized in "genius sperm." . . .

In their come-ons to buyers, sperm banks appeal simultaneously to popular eugenic hopes and the desire to match the characteristics of husbands and partners. Because they make available thousands of stored donor samples, purchasers can select from many possible combinations of characteristics. And those described in the catalog suggest what clients may be looking to acquire. Descriptive traits such as height, weight, hair color, eye color, and blood type are listed in all 27 donor catalogs examined. In addition, 23 banks provide information about "skin tone" (dark, olive, medium, light or fair; or in some instances "tanability"). Nineteen banks provide information about "hair texture" (wavy, straight, curly). Such traits are presumed to be heritable, that is, transmitted through genes, although there is no guarantee that a blue-eyed, blonde-haired donor, even when coupled with a blue-eyed, blonde-haired mother, will produce a blue-eyed, blonde-haired baby. In a process reminiscent of the discredited science of phrenology, Fairfax Cryobank in Virginia provides a detailed analysis of the "facial features" of donors, compartmentalizing the face into eyes (set, size, shape and shade), the nose (size width, length), the chin (prominence, cleft), the forehead (high or low hairline), and the overall shape of the face (square, oval or round). Some banks provide information about "dentition" of donors, with reports of impacted teeth or the donor's need for braces as a child. Some provide video or voice recordings or pictures of donors as babies. . . .

In Search of Better Babies

Eugenics practices of the early twentieth century emphasized differing reproductive, claims of the "fit" and the "unfit." Current sperm banking operations mirror, in modified form, such claims, now filtered through the presumably "neutral" mechanism of the marketplace. The attributes used to market "high quality" sperm—attributes of racial purity, physical prowess and intelligence—also become (or remain) idealized. Sperm banking and the popular eugenics of its clients combine to perpetuate the myth that desirable human traits are transmitted genetically, not socially, and that the traits most characteristic of certain races and social classes are the most desirable universal human traits. Sperm donors who are tall are more valuable than those who are short; the privately educated are privileged over those who attended vocational institutions; the fair-skinned are privileged over the dark; the fine-haired over the nappy. It is not just that consumers are disproportionately wealthy, well-educated or fair-skinned (although consumers are disproportionately white) and thus choosing donors like themselves. Within racial and ethnic categories, donors who "sell" reflect the idealized traits of the privileged white upper class—the tall, fair, slender, and "well-educated." In purchasing such semen, sperm banks and consumers engage in the commodification of social ideals. And too, they are counting on science to produce a superior product to the one that nature might offer.

The ideals and faith that sperm banks respond to are not late twentieth-century developments. They were part of AID from the very beginning. Physicians articulated the eugenic potential of AID and began the process by selecting donors of particular intellectual and social standing. The press, in turn, embraced the eugenic possibilities of AID because of prevailing faith in the science and because of the activities of medical specialists who promoted its advantages over "Dame Nature." Medical and popular faith that AID offered infertile couples both a solution to their individual problem and a means of bettering society pushed aside doubts about the legal status of the resulting offspring and overcame the moral uncertainties clouding the transaction. Offered the opportunity to select donors, doctors practiced office eugenics in obtaining sperm from donors whose contribution promised a "better baby." Later, practicing populist eugenics, consumers sought the same thing. In the case of sperm banking, eugenics was not simply an ideology imposed by an elite group nor a set of policies aimed at curtailing the reproduction of the unfit, it was a tool for presumably creating an ideal child by relying on what science, medicine, technology and ideology had to offer.

Amniocentesis Helps Detect Fetal Diseases

Rayna Rapp

Among the early developments in modern reproductive technology was amniocentesis, the extraction and analysis of fluid from the uterus of a pregnant woman. In the following selection anthropologist Rayna Rapp traces the roots of the procedure. First performed in 1882 as a way of relieving pressure in the womb, amniocentesis evolved into a method for detecting certain congenital diseases. By 1967 it had become possible to use amniocentesis to detect fetal genetic abnormalities such as Down syndrome, which gave women the option of aborting the fetus. Rayna Rapp is a professor of anthropology at New York University. She specializes in feminist biomedical issues.

Jerome Lejeune was not thinking about his enrollment in large-scale social transformations on that April day in 1958 when he peered through an aged microscope discarded by the bacteriology department at the Hopital Saint-Louis in Paris at a sample of smooth muscle tissue taken from three patients with Down syndrome. Lejeune, a French geneticist, and his cardiologist colleague Marthe Gauthier had used the innovative techniques of tissue culture to treat the sample. The full complement of human chromosomes had only been confirmed as forty-six in 1955–56. Lejeune was trying to assess whether his patients with Down syndrome lacked one human chromosome (as, by analogy, some abnormal fruit flies lacked one fruit fly chromosome). Instead, he (or, perhaps more accurately, he and Gauthier) discovered that they had a surfeit. Then, and in subsequent studies, tissue samples taken from people with Down syndrome yielded a chromosome count of forty-seven. With great hesitation, he published his results in 1959. At the same time, a research group at the University of Edinburgh independently arrived at the same findings, confirming the Paris research. As a provost at University College wrote to pioneering English geneticist Lionel Penrose upon hearing of these discoveries, "It must be one of the most important things that have happened in genetical studies for a long time."

From the Greeks On

Such "genetical studies" should be placed in a long philosophical and scientific genealogy that extends back to at least the Ancient Greeks. There, philosophers and healers speculated about the causes of generation, and the capacity of organisms to reproduce themselves. Influenced by the rediscovery of Hippocrates's materialism and Aristotle's concern with the fusion of form and matter, Early Modern natural philosophers attempted to resolve the debate between "epigenicists" and "preformationists": Did organisms develop progressively, from formless matter to fully formed entity, or were they present at Creation and at each of its iterations like little homunculi, already, fully shaped? Long before the modern science of genetics took disciplinary shape, eighteenth- and nineteenth-century concepts of inheritance were deeply rooted in the idea of estate or property transmission. As biology emerged as a field of study, "inheritance" was already freighted with a double meaning: it indexed both the structural properties of the organism and debates about that which constitutes it. A focus on both development and transmission comprised "genetic" thinking. This tension between developmental and iterative reproduction characterizes the history of biology and its daughter disciplines. Embryology, biochemistry, and physics all influenced the field of genetics, carrying a dualistic heritage of both linear or fixed replication and holistic, relational development with them.

Early scientific interest in developmental and transmissible inheritance had, of course, practical significance: Many of its most ardent students hailed from animal husbandry and agronomy, where experiments in hybridization were discussed under the rubric of "transmutation of species." The classic work of the Swede Carl Linnaeus had posited plant sexuality as the route to the production of new species via hybridity in the middle of the eighteenth century. He was followed by a long line of botanists who sought to prove experimentally that desirable characteristics could be successfully hybridized and retained across many generations. Opponents countered with theories of "reversion," observing that older, less desirable traits also reappeared across generations. Thus reversion and hybridization stood for a complex debate concerning the relative roles of nature and nurture, heredity and environment. The resolution of this problem would in part await the work of the Moravian monk Gregor Mendel, whose elegant mathematical ratios of pea traits across hybrid generations were published starting in 1865, but not "rediscovered" until the turn of the present century [the twentieth].

This long-standing scientific and agronomical interest in retention, reversion, and improvement of organic characteristics over the generations resonated through thinking about humans, as well as plants and animals. By the nineteenth century, a focus on the effects of the mother's imagination on the fetus gave way to a concern with consanguinity as a possible site of perfectibility and degeneration. Rapid urbanization in England and parts of the European continent also provided an anxious context for the study of degeneracy: It was widely presumed that civilization was both meliorable and degradable, and that properties such as propertylessness (pauperism, vagrancy, and associated ills like alcoholism and mental degeneracy) were transmissible across generations. Using methods from the evolving mathematical field of statistics in the later nineteenth century, [English physician] Francis Galton reconceptualized inheritance as a statistical relation between human populations of successive generations. In his bands, "inheritance" became "heredity" and was measured by "biometry," the statistical description of variable population characteristics ranging from height to intelligence, from "nomadism" to alcoholism. Galton's foundational influence on the international eugenics movement is anchored in this work. . . .

Gaining Knowledge of Genes

These scientific, practical, and sociological interests in inheritance resonated in the search for the actual entities through which intergenerational transmission might occur. Mendel's presentations of pea plant attributes across many generations of breeding were developed in his search for "factors" to explain plant traits; he made a strong case for the existence of a limited number of constant or "unit" characteristics that were carried by heritable material. By 1906, the English biologist William Bateson had coined the term "genetics" in his ardent attempts to substantiate both Darwin's and Mendel's work; in 1909, the Danish botanist Wilhelm Johannsen distinguished phenotype (external characteristics) from genotype (underlying hereditary units) carried by "genes." And the work of the American biologist T.H. Morgan brought together emergent techniques of cytologic microscopy and Mendelism in the study of fruit fly genetics in papers he published between 1911 and 1913. The material substances Morgan actually studied were not "genes" but "chromosomes," those threadlike structures which are visible with the use of a microscope. By enrolling drosophila and their conveniently short generations to the project of scientific inquiry, chromosomal variation could be bred and manipulated under laboratory conditions. Morgan, along with the English zoologist Lyell Darlington, established that unit characteristics visible in the organism were passed on together or separately at different rates, depending on their location on chromosomes. This work also directed researchers to the study of sex-limited (now called X-linked) characteristics as a prime locus of genetic investigation. For Morgan, Darlington, and their followers, the study of chromosomes in germ-cell nuclei was the key to genetic discoveries. And, according to Morgan, "In the same sense in which the chemist posits invisible atoms and the physicist electrons, the student of heredity appeals to invisible elements called genes."

Focus on Chromosomes

Across the Atlantic, the German zoologists August Weismann and Oscar Hertwig also used cytology to study germ-line cells, but they rejected "nuclear monopolies" in favor of a more interactive theory of the cytoplasm (extranuclear cellular material): Once again, the debate between fixed entities carrying the instructions for reproduction and a more relational theory of organelle, organ, and organismic development preoccupied many scientists.

By the time of World War I, the international European and American collaborative effort to study genetics had come of age. Its focus was on sexual reproduction via reduction division involving chromosomes; its objects of study were chromosomes on which still invisible but posited genes were "known" to be lodged; its methods were at once microbiological, biochemical, and statistical. While the highly visible chromosome quickly became an international consensus object of scientific investigation, genes have had a more checkered history: To this day, scientific debates about the relation of genetic information and organismic development remain intense, replaying earlier scientific controversies in a molecular register. It is within this international collaborative scholarly network and its debates that Lejeune's discovery should be situated.

First Amniocentesis

A few years later, in 1967, American researchers reported the first detection of a fetal chromosome problem in a sample of fluid drawn from the amniotic sac inside the womb of a pregnant woman. Amniocentesis—the technique of extracting amniotic fluid transabdominally through a hollow catheter—was first performed and described in Germany in 1882 by a doctor attempting to relieve harmful pressure on the fetus of a pregnant woman. It became an experimental treatment for polyhydramnios (excess fetal fluid which threatened fetal development), but was not widely used until the 1950s, when researchers in Great Britain and the United States discovered they could deploy the same technique to test for maternal-fetal blood group incompatibility and to assess the severity of Rh disease. In critical cases, amniocentesis led to intrauterine transfusion. It also led to the assessment of fetal lung maturity, so that fetuses with serious disease could be delivered as early, and as safely, as possible.

The treatment of polyhydramnios and Rh disease established familiarity with amniocentesis as an invasive technique. Advances in prenatal diagnosis awaited the development of technologies that isolated, cultured, and characterized chromosomes in amniotic fluid. That story begins with the discovery of sex chromatin—the inactivated somatic cell X chromosome, or barr body, distinguishing females from males in humans—which was characterized in the late 1940s and early '50s. Its discovery paved the way for experiments in Minneapolis, New York, Copenhagen, and Haifa to predict fetal sex via amniocentesis. Some of the earliest experimental "fishing expeditions" inside women's wombs were undertaken on mothers who already had a son with hemophilia and wanted to know the sex of the fetus. If it was determined to be chromosomally male, then they ran a 50 percent risk of having another son affected by the disease. In 1960, an obstetrical team in Copenhagen reported the first abortion after the determination of male fetal sex in a carrier of hemophilia. By the time that researchers in Sweden, Denmark, Great Britain, and the United States began experimenting more widely with amniotic prenatal diagnosis for Down syndrome and other chromosomal conditions, the technology to invade the uterus, extract its liquids, and characterize fetal chromosomes was an international project. It had enrolled not only researcher-clinicians from several continents but mothers of "blue babies" and hemophiliac sons in its experimental development.

Combined with Ultrasound

The evolution of amniocentesis was accompanied by closely related international developments. In the same year that Lejeune observed the chromosomes of his Down syndrome patients in France, midwifery professor Ian Donald and his colleagues in Glasgow published an article called the "Investigation of Abdominal Masses by Pulsed Ultrasound." In it, they described the adaptation of sonar technology—originally developed during World War I for detecting enemy submarines—to the detection of fetuses inside their mother's wombs. . . .

As many feminists have pointed out, the technology intervened in the doctor-patient relationship dramatically, allowing the physician to bypass pregnant women's self-reports in favor of a "window" on the developing fetus. Additionally, radiologists and obstetricians working together could use sonograms in the developing technology of amniocentesis. It enabled them to picture where the fetus wasn't, and the fluid was, rather than groping blindly for a pocket of liquid into which to insert the amnio-bound catheter. As "real time" sonography became available, the technology allowed doctors to observe a moving image of the fetus while sampling its environment. When used in conjunction with sonography, experimental invasive techniques of the womb became safer, and the miscarriage rates attributable to these procedures dropped dramatically.

The technology of prenatal diagnosis continues to evolve at a rapid pace.

The World's First Test-Tube Baby

Robert Edwards and Patrick Steptoe

In vitro fertilization (IVF) has become a common procedure for women whose fallopian tubes are blocked. The technique is straightforward: An egg is surgically removed from the patient and fertilized with sperm before being inserted into the womb. In the following selection the two men responsible for IVF describe their efforts to bring IVF to fruition. Patrick Steptoe and Robert Edwards recount the culmination of their campaign. The breakthrough came with Lesley and John Brown, one of three infertile couples that Steptoe and Edwards were treating at a small private hospital in northern England. On July 25, 1978, Lesley Brown gave birth to a healthy girl. Louise Joy Brown was hailed in the media as the world's first test-tube baby. Patrick Steptoe was a gynecologist and a leading fertility expert. He died in 1988. Robert Edwards is a biomedical researcher.

I parked the car outside Kershaw's [hospital]. Then walked carefully, because of the slippery damp leaves on the pathway, into the little hospital where [scientist] Bob [Edwards] and [technician] Jean [Purdy] were waiting for me. Bob had phoned me earlier, urging me to come over and see this new method of measuring the LH [luteinizing hormone] surge. 'This Hi-Gonavis [ovulation testing] is a beautifully packed kit. Typical Japanese ingenuity,' he had said. I was confronted with a series of little tubes full of red blood cells. They were scattered everywhere from the mantelpiece to the window sills.

Bob and Jean felt confident that they would now be able to tell me exactly when a laparoscopy would be worthwhile—

their judgement based on the results of these little tubes. Weeks before they had squabbled about the best way of doing things. Now they had made up their minds and I was faced with their united view. The procedure could be awkward. It would no longer be possible to carry out operations when it suited me or my team. But Bob and Jean knew that Muriel Harris, my [surgical] theatre supervisor, along with my anaesthetists and my nurses, would stand by me in any demand that I should make upon them. They were right. I was lucky to enjoy such generous loyalty.

One of the patients waiting for a laparoscopy at Kershaw's that autumn day was Lesley Brown. They had been testing samples of her urine as well as those of other patients with the Hi-Gonavis kits, and on 10 November 1977 at 11 A.M., twenty-six hours after the onset of her LH surge had been identified on the fifteenth day of her cycle, she was ready for laparoscopy. At the same time, [husband] John Brown produced a fresh semen specimen.

Clean sterile air was pumped into the laboratory and the preparation of a warm stage on the microscope completed. John's semen was examined and by spinning it in a centrifuge the spermatozoa separated from their plasma. The latter was removed and a carefully prepared culture medium put in its place. The concentration of spermatozoa was so adjusted that one millilitre of the mixture contained one million sperms. Droplets of the prepared semen were now placed under liquid paraffin in a Petri dish and then put in an incubator kept at normal body temperature. The vessel holding the Petri dish was capable of being filled with a special gas mixture which could maintain the balance between alkalinity and acidity— otherwise the sperm cells would be damaged. So John's spermatozoa were ready. Now we needed to recover the one ovum of Lesley's that was presumably ripening and ready to be collected.

Extraction of the Egg

Lesley had been anaesthetized by Dr Finlay Campbell. My assistant, Dr John Webster, had completed his preparations for the laparoscopy and now we were ready to begin. Lesley had been draped and a special needle was passed into the abdomen at the lower border of her navel so that a gas mixture, the same as that used for fertilization and cleavage, could be passed into the abdomen while the operating table was tilted head downwards about 20 degrees. The gas in the pelvis allowed a free safe space for larger instruments to be introduced while the intestines fell back out of the way.

When I introduced the laparoscope I could see that there had been some recurrence of adhesions around the ovaries despite the operative treatment given earlier to Lesley. Another instrument was introduced from the side of the abdomen and the womb and ovaries were mobilized by holding the supporting ligaments and by manipulating them. My heart sank. The right ovary contained three small follicles only. No pre-ovulatory follicle was there. Had Bob and Jean's estimations, with the help of the Hi-Gonavis kit, been wrong? Bob was no more than eight feet away from me on the other side of the door which separated the operating theatre from the culture laboratory. We had recently established an intercommunication system and I was tempted to say out loud my disappointment. But first I would view the left ovary which I was finding more difficult to mobilize. I had to remove carefully a small omental adhesion. And then—ah there it was, I could see it!—a ripe, pinkish-blue follicle. Yes, on the under surface of that left ovary a good ripe follicle about three centimetres in diameter.

'Bob, one good follicle in the left ovary,' I said, pleased, over the intercom. 'But not easy to approach. Adhesions.'

'I'm ready,' Bob replied.

To the left of the midline I introduced a sharp cannula some 2.2 millimetres in diameter. I then injected through it some anti-clot saline solution which would clean away any minute traces of fat and blood that might have entered it. Through the cleaned cannula I introduced a special long needle, 1.3 millimetres in diameter, which was attached to a collecting glass chamber by a tube. This, in turn, was joined to an electric aspirating pump controlled by Muriel Harris. I quickly steered the needle to the follicle and pierced its wall from the side. 'Right,' I said to Muriel who, under my direction, applied suction. I watched the follicle slowly empty drop by drop into the collecting system. It was beautiful—a slow collapse of the follicle and a clear amber fluid collecting in the glass chamber.

'Stop!' I commanded.

After the chamber was detached from the suction system and a sterile lid placed on it, a nurse carried the precious cargo to the hatch between the theatre and the culture laboratory where Jean received it. She would pass it carefully on to Bob to examine under a microscope, having already put the semen droplets in their dish on the warmed stage. While I waited for Bob's verdict I placed a new glass chamber in position.

'Got it,' I heard Bob say. 'An excellent egg. Just right, I'm happy.'

Mixing Egg and Sperm

Bob washed the egg through the culture media using a pipette which he controlled by finger and thumb pressure on a small rubber bulb. I have always admired Bob's skill in using these pipettes. How easily he picked up an egg to transfer it from one droplet to another without losing it—all under microscopic vision.

Now we were working separately. While he was placing the washed egg in a droplet of culture with some 20,000 spermatozoa in it, I, in the operating theatre, was withdrawing the aspirating needle. The diminutive hole in the follicle did not bleed. I took out the cannula and holding forceps. The gas was evacuated and replaced by carbon dioxide. This helped to clear out the other special gas which otherwise would have only been absorbed slowly. Then the carbon dioxide itself was emptied out and the laparoscope withdrawn. Finally I closed the two small incisions with tantalum clips. The operation was over. Within fifteen minutes of the anaesthetic being started Lesley was awake and ready to be wheeled back to her bed.

'Did you get an egg?' she asked me softly.

'Yes, a very nice egg. You can go back to sleep.'

Mrs Brown slept for a few hours. At four o'clock that day she was sitting up happily taking her tea, and later that evening she was out of bed and walking around a little. It had hardly been a major ordeal. Meanwhile the egg and the sperms were in the incubator. By ten o'clock that same night fertilization had occurred. . . .

Bob and Jean examined the embryo. . . . At last it had eight cells. I took a brief glimpse at it. It was beautiful, eight rounded, perfect cells. The cumulus cells had broken away and I was filled with awe at the loveliness of this minuscule dot of potential human life. It was time to change into my hospital blues and to move Lesley Brown into the theatre so that I could replace this same vibrant dot into the body of her womb.

As I changed I plunged my face into ice-cold water. Lesley was now in the theatre in position. It was not long before I unveiled the sterile tray that had been previously prepared by Muriel Harris. Bob stood by, gowned and gloved. I put together the little plastic cannula and syringe, then handed it to him. He went to the adjacent lab to load the precious embryo into the end of the cannula under microscopic control. This step required nerves of steel. And while Bob was doing this I covered Lesley with sterile green towels and gently exposed the entrance to her womb.

'Are you comfortable?' I asked Lesley.

'Yes.'

I gently swabbed the cervix with some warm culture fluid—the entrance to it was clean and healthy. Now we waited. Lesley Brown and I waited for Bob and Jean. We had to wait two long minutes. At last Bob was at my side holding the loaded tube and syringe in two hands. I guided the syringe towards the entrance with my left hand and the tube, firmly in the grip of long dissecting forceps, with my right hand. Forwards and inwards to the opening into which mercifully the smoothed end of the tube slid. We held steady. Together Bob and I advanced the precious load into the body of the womb.

'We're right,' I said to Bob.

Jean was watching anxiously. Bob gently advanced the plunger so as to expel the embryo from the cannula into the womb. We hoped that now the tiny droplet carrying the embryo had passed into the lining folds of the womb. Bob released the syringe and tube entirely into my care and I held steady for one, two minutes before slowly, cautiously, withdrawing the tube. Bob hovered close by, ready to receive the whole apparatus as soon as it was free. It came out gently. I watched the lips of the cervix close without any sign of fluid being rejected from it. Bob took the syringe and tube back to the lab microscope. Jean joined him. They had to make sure the embryo had left the tube.

'All right, Lesley?'

'Fine.'

She seemed relaxed and confident, and soon Jean's smiling eyes above her mask and her upraised thumb indicated that all was well. I removed the instrument, releasing Lesley from her uncomfortable position. We moved her gently from the operating table to the trolley and then on to her bed where she was tucked up for the night. As Jean bent over her Mrs Brown remarked, 'That was a wonderful experience.' It seemed she was sure that now she really had started her baby.

CHAPTER 2

Modern Reproductive Technologies

The Burgeoning Assisted Reproduction Industry

Anna Mulrine

The use of in vitro fertilization (IVF) carries various risks, but the popularity of the procedure is soaring. In the following selection Anna Mulrine describes the emotional and financial burdens that many infertile couples incur in their effort to have a baby. Focusing on one clinic based in Las Vegas, Nevada, Mulrine notes that most of the couples patronizing the Sher Institutes for Reproductive Medicine fly in from out of state. As IVF has a 70 percent failure rate, most have to make repeated trips. Between travel costs and medical fees, couples run up bills that can total in the hundreds of thousands of dollars. For those who succeed, Mulrine observes, the expense and effort seem worthwhile. However, some studies suggest that children born via IVF may suffer higher rates of health problems later in life than children conceived naturally. Despite the risks, one in a hundred children born in the United States is conceived through IVF. Anna Mulrine writes on health and medical issues for U.S. News & World Report.

It is implantation day for some of the toughest cases at the Sher Institutes for Reproductive Medicine in Las Vegas. The couples that pass through this place, headquarters for one of the largest chains of infertility clinics in America, are seasoned pros in the quest to make babies. They have tried shots and surrogates and have graduated to advanced treatments beyond their wildest calculations. Most of them have already undergone two or more in vitro fertilization [IVF] attempts with other doctors, and some 75 percent of them have traveled from out of state to try again. It is an arduous process, not

Anna Mulrine, "Making Babies," *U.S. News & World Report*, September 27, 2004, pp. 1–6.

without its embarrassments. One couple speaks of feeling ridiculous racing through rush-hour traffic to deliver sperm gathered at home to the clinic; another describes an earlier treatment when the doctor, in a lame effort at humor, dressed in a bunny suit on egg retrieval day, in preparation for his "Easter hunt."

It is also expensive. The couples in this waiting room have spent tens—and hundreds—of thousands of dollars on infertility treatments. They have gambled big, won, and lost. Robert and Bernadette from Fort Lauderdale, Fla., have spent $200,000 so far on doctors and medicine, and are back in the city for another IVF attempt. They have flown so often to Las Vegas that a friend unaware of their plight confronted them because he feared they had a serious gambling problem. "In a way," Robert ventures, "we do."

A Growth Industry

It is indeed a gamble but one an increasing number of couples are willing to take. A quarter century after the first "test tube" baby, the use of assisted reproductive technology (ART) has risen astronomically. In the past decade alone, the number of ART babies has quadrupled, from 10,924 in 1994 to 40,687 in 2001, the most recent figure available. Today [2004] 1 in 100 children in this country is conceived with such treatments, but the industry itself remains largely unregulated, sparking calls for more rigorous reporting of data and more research on the possible risks of ART.

But the rewards are great—the joys of parenthood make any sacrifice seem worthwhile to the many childless couples passing through the Sher Institutes' doors.

Take Steven and Mary Crespi. They have a daughter, Jay-Cee, 2, from a previous IVF attempt. Etched beneath a heart tattooed on Steven's arm is Daddy's Girl. Now they're trying for a sibling. When Mary, 40, miscarried twins during her last IVF pregnancy, Steven, a bartender and host at a club in town, was devastated. "He didn't talk for two days," says Mary. Steven nods vigorously. "I didn't." For almost a year, Mary adds, "he's been really angry." Steven nods again, this time more slowly. "I swore," he says, "that I would never. Do this. Again." And yet, they have taken out a second mortgage on their house and are back at Sher.

So are Irene and her husband, Peter, from Chicago. They estimate they have spent nearly $300,000 on several surrogates as well as IVF. In their case, medical insurance paid half of their IVF bills, a rarity in the United States, where 85 percent of insured Americans have policies that will not cover that treatment. Over the past several years, Irene and Peter have had three IVF treatments per year. Today they are tense as they file out of the room where Irene's eggs, fertilized with her husband's sperm, have just been implanted in their surrogate. Irene had wanted four eggs implanted, to increase the odds of a success, while her husband wanted three, to decrease the chances of the complications that come with multiple births. They argued, but Irene prevailed, and now she clutches a photograph of one of their newly fertilized eggs. As its cells have divided, it has grown to look like a beautiful flower, she says. Peter disagrees. "What it looks like," he says from his seat on the other side of the waiting room, "is a nuclear bomb."

Questions About Risks for Offspring

For the estimated 1 in 6 American couples trying unsuccessfully to have a child each year, that's just what infertility can be, as they put their relationships, their finances, and, perhaps, their family's health on the line to make a baby. Indeed, there remains surprisingly little agreement about the future health implications on the offspring that parents are trying so desperately to create through ART. "I started reading the literature, and pretty soon I was completely confused," says Kathy Hudson, director of the Genetics and Public Policy Center at Johns Hopkins University. A molecular biologist who formerly served as the assistant director of the Human Genome Project at the National Institutes of Health, Hudson encountered studies that seemed to indicate that there were slightly higher rates of birth defects, cancer, and genetic diseases associated with certain IVF techniques. Others seemed to point to no difference at all. "I couldn't tell you whether IVF kids run faster and jump higher than their non-IVF peers or not," Hudson says. In a significant step to begin bridging that knowledge gap, the center, in partnership with the American Society of Reproductive Medicine and the American Academy of Pediatrics, will next present the most comprehensive study yet undertaken to examine the impact of ART on the health of children.[1]

It's a vital undertaking, as the business of infertility gets bigger and more complicated. Spending on IVF alone is up 50 percent in the past five years, to over $1 billion [in 2003]. What's more, incentives such as multiple IVF attempts for one fee and money-back guarantees (the Sher clinic offers up to 100 percent off for failed IVF attempts) are bringing patients to clinics in greater numbers than ever before.

But increasingly, doctors, expert advisers to the government, and the patients themselves are wondering what, exactly, would-be parents are getting for their money. Statistics surrounding reproductive technologies can be confusing. "It is impossible to know how many individuals undergo assisted reproduction procedures in a given year, how many patients achieve success in the first (or second or third) cycle, how many women fail to conceive," the President's Council on Bioethics said in a report released [in 2004]. The concern is centered on figures collected by the Society for Assisted Reproductive Technology—the accrediting body for reproductive physicians—mandated by law in 1992 and published since

1. The report, according to a Johns Hopkins Medical Center news release, found no evidence of increased risk of most malformations, cancer or impaired psychosocial development. However, it found that individual IVF babies are at increased risk for low birth weight, prematurity, and perinatal mortality. It also found that multiple births, which carry additional risks, are ten times more likely to occur through IVF.

1996 by the Centers for Disease Control and Prevention. "I think there are a host of changes that you could make to make the [reporting] process more rigorous, in terms of protecting consumers," says Sen. Ron Wyden, a Democrat from Oregon who wrote the first legislation.

Slow to Meet Demand

Reproductive medicine has been stung by controversy from the start. A century ago, physicians reacted to news of the first artificial insemination in 1909 with equal parts outrage and disbelief. Even if the news was true—though that, they tended to agree, was highly unlikely—it was sure to be "ridiculously criminal." When a wealthy Philadelphia couple entered the offices of a well-regarded physician in 1884, desperate to have a baby, the husband privately confessed to battling a bout of gonorrhea. The doctor decided to take matters in his own hands, writes Robin Marantz Henig in *Pandora's Baby: How the First Test Tube Babies Sparked the Reproductive Revolution.* He tapped the best-looking member of his class of medical students to provide sperm and injected it into his anesthetized patient. Some nine months later, the couple welcomed a baby boy into the world. It was not until after the child was born to the couple that the doctor told the husband the truth. The man was unfazed but made the doctor promise not to tell his wife.

Still, for decades, desire for children far outpaced the medical community's ability to do anything about it. "Even as man walked on the moon, no one knew when a woman ovulated," said Dr. Robert Edwards, the British fertility pioneer who delivered the world's first test-tube baby, Louise Brown, in July 1978.

Today science has caught up. In the lab at the Sher Institutes, Madonna's "Like a Prayer" is playing on the radio as the lab technicians cut the tails off sperm to keep them from darting away. They are drawn up into a thin needle and injected directly into the eggs of their patients; this procedure is known as ICSI [intracytoplasmic sperm injection]. Then the technicians and the patients wait. Couples know in about three days whether their incubating eggs will be good enough to implant.

Hunt for Good Eggs

On the other side of the wall, Mary Crespi has taken a Valium, and her bladder is full, to better prepare her body for implantation. She and Steven also had sex the night before, as they had been encouraged by their doctor to do. It was not easy, she says, with her anxiety about today and his bad back. She's wearing Steven's jacket—it's cold in the operating room—and the same socks she wore the day her eggs were retrieved. Steven carries a letter he has written to their fertilized eggs. "I can't wait to meet you," it reads. "Go give me my babies," Steven cheers. Mary tells Steven that he's making her nervous. Steven starts praying. Mary tries to relax. "I look nicer when I'm pregnant," she muses.

Mary's chances of conceiving today are a long shot. Even in the best circumstances, at age 40—Mary's age—specialists estimate that between 40 and 70 percent of women's eggs show evidence of abnormalities. Of the nine eggs that doctors were able to harvest and fertilize, three will be implanted today. Six more of Mary's eggs will continue to grow, and with any luck, one or two will make it to the blastocyst, or 108-cell stage. They will then be frozen for later use. Generally, fewer than a third of all eggs make it that far.

Their doctor enters the room and hugs Steven. He is Geoffrey Sher, the founder and medical director of the institutes. Then a window that connects the lab and the operating room slides open. Through it, a technician passes a catheter filled with Mary and Steven's fertilized eggs. The implantation is over in a couple of minutes. Mary hugs her knees to her chest—she will remain lying down for about a half-hour.

73

"These are gorgeous embryos. Absolutely gorgeous," Sher assures them. "They don't make them any better."

The perfect egg. Looks, however, matter less than once thought. In the past, reproductive specialists would score eggs based on criteria like smooth cell walls and good symmetry. But they were often surprised—eggs that seemed quite attractive simply stopped growing, and those that appeared to be duds became healthy babies nine months later. They simply didn't know what made some embryos develop and others not. Now they have more than an inkling. In a paper published in the journal *Reproductive BioMedicine Online . . .*, researchers at the Sher Institutes announced that they had discovered a genetic marker in the fluid surrounding each embryo—a molecule called sHLA-G that is produced by the embryo during pregnancy. "We can now look at an embryo," says Sher, "and say if that marker is present" there is a 70 percent chance that it will make a baby in women under age 39 and an over 50 percent chance in women 39 to 44 years old. "It's huge, huge," he adds. "This system is going to allow us to have one baby, one woman."

That's because the better the accuracy in predicting embryo viability, the fewer embryos that need to be implanted in patients in the first place. And that brings reproductive specialists closer to their holy grail: the birth of a single healthy baby. Indeed, it is multiples that pose the single greatest risk to the health of patients and families using assisted reproductive technologies, says Marcelle Cedars, the director of reproductive endocrinology and infertility at the University of California–San Francisco. And though there has been a decline in the number of cases of three or more fetuses carried by IVF patients, twin births are still on the rise.

The Price of Pregnancy

Having a better handle on which embryos will make healthy pregnancies would help to bring down costs of IVF as well.

The majority of infertile couples who seek treatment conceive through drug regimens like Clomid or intrauterine insemination—insurance companies generally insist that their clients exhaust these avenues before they move on to IVF. For many infertile couples, the size of their pocketbook determines whether they can have a family, says Diane Clapp, the medical information director at Resolve, a nationwide infertility association. Indeed, for the roughly 1 million patients per year who would benefit from IVF, some 120,000 receive it, according to Sher. And with a 70 percent average failure rate per IVF attempt, most patients need more than a single treatment—which can cost anywhere from $7,000 to $15,000. Robert and Bernadette from Fort Lauderdale paid out of pocket for their IVF regimen after Bernadette had a negative reaction to Clomid. The Crespis, too, are paying for IVF treatment on their own. Sher sees many patients who "are really mauled. They're financially and emotionally bankrupt by the time they end up with you." But he says insurance companies are not to blame; it's the industry that needs to grow more accountable. "Until we get our house in order," Sher says, it is understandable that coverage is not forthcoming. He would like someday to see insurance coverage that provides incentives for fertility clinics, with penalties for triplets and bonuses for single, healthy births, he says.

It is also an industry that bears the burden of its association with controversial stem cell research and cloning. Since much infertility research falls into the category of research on embryos, the National Institutes of Health is largely prevented from underwriting experiments in reproductive science—a restriction that robs the field of an oversight process. "We hear people whining and yapping about it and trying to blame the IVF medical practice," says Elizabeth Blackburn, a cell biologist and professor at the University of California–San Francisco, who served on the bioethics council. "On the other hand, well, hello, there hasn't been federal funding, dummies, and federal funding is a very good mechanism because it has built into it transparency and peer review." In its absence, the industry is often described as a medical Wild West—with its share of snake oil salesmen.

Risks of Emotional Trauma

But perhaps the biggest risk of all for couples embarking on reproductive therapies is the emotional backlash they often experience. Alice Domar, director of the Mind/Body Center for Women's Health at Boston IVF and an assistant professor of obstetrics, gynecology, and reproductive biology at Harvard Medical School, has seen couples who blame themselves for being infertile—for being too selfish, for waiting too long to start a family. She has counseled worried wives convinced that their husbands will leave them for a fertile woman.

"Men and women respond to infertility very differently," says Domar. "Women who have never been jealous a day in their lives may all of a sudden get unbelievably jealous when someone else gets pregnant. And the husband may respond, 'Ew, what's wrong with you? You're jealous that my sister's pregnant.'" At the Mind/Body Center, men often meet with male therapists to vent. "They need to hear that their wife is normal, that she's not being a basket case," says Domar.

Steven and Mary Crespi say that while it has been a grueling experience, it has also brought them closer as a couple, as a family. Domar says studies have found that despite the considerable strain, the divorce rate in infertile couples is lower than in married couples with children.

But in the thick of treatment, it is hard not to feel overwhelmed. Irene and Peter are worried because not one of their four embryos implanted that afternoon in the clinic became a viable pregnancy. Several weeks later, their surrogate walked out of the process in the middle of another attempt—after Irene had paid to fly her to Vegas and had spent nearly $20,000 for insurance and other medical expenses. Irene vows to keep trying. "Until I go through menopause, I need to exhaust this option," she says.

As for Robert and Bernadette from Fort Lauderdale, they married last December [2003], in the hopes that God might look more favorably on their attempts to make a baby as husband and wife.

But after two tries, the Crespis' struggle to have a second baby is looking up. Days after the implantation, they have good news—Mary's progesterone levels have shot up from 15 to 51 in two days. She's not feeling any morning sickness, she says, in a voice that sounds disappointed; then she reminds herself that she rarely felt queasy when she was carrying her daughter, either. Two weeks later, they have an ultrasound, and they know for sure. They will have a baby boy. "Our family is complete," says Mary. "And you know what? I don't want to go through this again."

Prenatal Genetic Screenings and Their Risks

Roger Gosden

Historically, assisted reproduction focused on helping infertile couples get pregnant, notes Roger Gosden. In the following selection Gosden describes how assisted reproductive technologies have now expanded to include techniques that allow doctors to screen embryos for genetic defects. Prenatal genetic screening gives a woman the option of forgoing implantation of an embryo if the tests indicate that the embryo has genetic defects. Furthermore, Gosden observes, new genetic technologies are likely to provide the capacity to correct defects or insert enhancements into a developing fetus. The combination of genetic screening and genetic enhancement has a troubling side, Gosden concludes. Parents may be tempted to try to concoct a "superman" or "superwoman," he notes. McGill University Medical School professor Roger Gosden is an expert in reproductive biology. He trained with Robert Edwards, a pioneer of in vitro fertilization.

Ignorance and superstition about infertility were the norms in prudish Victorian society that forbade sex education and research. Children's curiosity about their origins was brushed aside with diversions and anecdotes about birds and bees, storks, and gooseberry bushes: consequently children learned from one another—and often a lot of nonsense. The world of academia was not much more enlightened, and fertility research remained a stagnant backwater for a long time. Even such fundamental facts as the time in the month when a woman ovulates were unknown until the 1930s, and family planning methods were correspondingly ineffective. Medical practitioners could offer little help to people wanting to turn the fertility tap on or off and, feeling helpless, tended to avoid such questions. In 1930s Britain, one woman wrote to women's rights campaigner Marie Stopes, "We had a talk with our own doctor but he appeared unwilling to speak about it, so we did not pursue the matter further." Children were still regarded as "gifts," and, though they arrived at frequent intervals in some families, unluckier couples had meekly to accept their infertility and deny instincts and expectations that others assumed to be their birthright.

The Dawn of Family Planning

After shocking the British public with the candor of her book *Married Love,* published at the end of World War I, Marie Stopes delivered a series of boisterous lectures and founded clinics up and down the country promoting sexual health and family planning. Here, at last, was an advocate for couples who were suffering from an excess or want of reproduction and who dearly hoped to bring their fruitfulness under control. Once the social inhibitions began to lift and more effective methods of fertility control were available, couples started to choose when to have children according to their preferences and circumstances, rather than leaving matters to nature.

The ambition to have a family is still strong in most people, despite the falling birth rate, and it first emerges in our nursery days when we play mothers and fathers. When our make-believe days are over, there are social pressures on top of the old biological urges to try the real thing. Would-be grandparents, aunts, and uncles welcome family additions and can be relied on to drop a few hints to an older couple "before it is too late." Everyone seems to be proud and gain status when a planned child arrives, and, in return, parents hope to win some reciprocal affection from their offspring and some security in old age. Perhaps those who have been denied children recognize the urge better than those who take their fertility for granted. Indeed, the strength of this urge has a biblical authority. God commanded Noah to "go forth and multiply," and Noah begat three sons; many Christian church wedding services still beseech the happy couple to be "fruitful."

On top of all these factors, there is something ineffable about the longing to be someone's parent. After self-preservation and satisfying hunger this is the most fundamental urge, and obviously it is vital for the species. Even the asexual amoeba has to split in two or face extinction. We seldom think this way, but reproduction is the only bid we can make for a small slice of immortality—through the survival of our genes, that is. Whatever heights of achievement we attain in our careers, whatever public acclaim we enjoy, most of us will be forgotten in a couple of generations. But our genes endure in our descendants, even though each set is shuffled and only half of them are passed down to each son and daughter. The "pack" has hardly changed at all over eons of time, and the urge to perpetuate the genes is powerful and universal and wells up from our Stone Age past.

The Age of Assisted Reproduction

The first timid step taken by science to treat infertility was carried out by [Scottish physician] John Hunter, but it took another 200 years before a major stride was made. If pressed to state the time and place of this breakthrough, I would say that it came just after midnight on July 25, 1978, in a small hospital in Oldham, Lancashire. After years of trying, the Brown family produced Louise, the first baby conceived by in vitro fertilization. She was born after a decade of research endeavor by the gynecologist Patrick Steptoe and the Cambridge physiologist Robert Edwards, and she emerged into a world full of curiosity about her.

The two men had to conquer not only the difficult problem of conception and growing embryos in a culture fluid, but also fierce opposition, even from their medical colleagues. It was feared, even by some fellow professionals, that interfering with a natural process would produce monsters, and the Frankenstein story was duly trotted out in the newspapers. Signaling their doubts, the much-respected *New York Times* ran the headline "Brave New Baby," and *Time* magazine called the Cambridge laboratory "Orwell's baby farm," implying something unsavory about laboratory conception. Rather than rejoicing at the birth of a healthy baby girl to parents who had made enormous sacrifices, the daring experiment was condemned, and it was feared that a Pandora's box of "human hatcheries" had been opened.

In the years since the breakthrough, assisted reproductive technology (ART) has evolved into a conventional treatment. Nearly 0.2% of American and 1% of British babies are being born after IVF, which is just one form of ART. There are now more than 300,000 IVF babies worldwide. Patients stand in line for treatment, regardless of the stress, discomfort, and risks and despite the fact that the success rate for the treatment is seldom better than 1 in 5. The lengths to which some people will go to have the child they desperately want reveal more clearly than anything else how powerfully we are driven by our desire to carry forward our own kind.

Reproductive technology did not stand still for long before moving forward with another innovation. Originally developed to bypass blocked fallopian tubes so that the embryo can reach the womb, IVF has turned out to be useful for treating all sorts of problems, in males as well as in females. New methods are constantly being invented to help the process of conception. Spare embryos can be frozen at minimal cost, and, since the first little "frosties"—as the first babies who were born from frozen embryos were known—arrived in the mid-1980s, most clinics now offer this service. Egg donation was developed for women whose ovaries are prematurely barren, and it has turned out to be effective for women of more mature years. Biopsies from embryos can be genetically screened for heritable diseases before transferring the embryos to the womb to ensure a healthy baby and avoiding the decision to abort a defective fetus later on. A chance discovery in a laboratory led to another revolutionary treatment (not cure) for men with low sperm counts. Injecting a sperm directly into an egg, a technique called intracytoplasmic sperm injection (ICSI), enables even the most underendowed male to father a child, and it has swept through IVF centers to become standard practice. Such lightning progress causes people to wonder how far the technology will have gone in a few more years' time.

Social Changes Underway

Whereas our parents' generation left matters to nature, we take fertility for granted. Few people of any age need now be involuntarily infertile. If the time-honored methods fail, the problem usually has a technological solution. Consequently, we have come to regard parenthood as more of a right than a privilege and a right that can be exercised at our behest and in the circumstances of our choosing. The majority of family units in the West are still of the nuclear variety—Mom, Dad, and the kids, like the Brown family—but immense social changes are underway. In vitro fertilization, gamete donation (egg or sperm), and surrogacy open the door to previously undreamed-of choices, including solo or homosexual parenthood as well as motherhood past the age of 50. These are just some of the unintended consequences of scientific advances, and there will be many more in the future.

Such possibilities provoke strong reactions, and as a result, reproductive medicine in some countries has become hedged about with more legislation and regulation than any other branch of medicine. The main concern has been to safeguard the interests of children, although surprisingly few problems have emerged so far. Attitudes are likely to harden as ART moves on from infertility treatment to more effective prenatal screening and selection and then, possibly, to genetic enhancement. As we strive to make our lives as painless and secure as possible, it is natural to want to remove the uncertainties about pregnancy and our offspring, too.

Poor-Quality Embryos

Reproduction has always been a risky business, and many embryos perish naturally in the womb before the woman even realizes she is pregnant. Some reproductive waste can be reduced by improving health during pregnancy, but little can be done, as yet, about the large numbers of poor-quality embryos that are the cause of many a miscarriage. No other mammal we know of is as prodigal with its seed or has a higher frequency of birth defects. Most of the prenatal losses are "merciful" because the embryos are chromosomally abnormal, and any large imbalance in the number of genes always has some harmful effects. Why the germ cells are so much more susceptible to abnormalities than the rest of the body is a mystery, but usually only the fittest embryos stand a good chance of going the whole distance of pregnancy. Nevertheless, occasionally an abnormal embryo is strong enough to escape the selection process and is born with a defect.

Before the advent of prenatal screening there was no reliable way of telling whether a baby would be normal or not. Pregnancy screening and fetal diagnosis now give a mother information to help her decide whether to take further tests or even have a medical termination. As technology advances, more and more information about the baby will become available. The prospect of screening the entire genome at the embryo stage is not very far off. But the closer we look, the more "flaws" we are likely to find. What should our reaction be? Should we help the natural screening process that eliminates most defective fetuses as miscarriages, and, if so, who should decide? Must we not acknowledge that none of us is perfect and wonder who would meet the strictest criteria? It is not always easy to define abnormality, but there may sometimes be value in it. The Norwegian expressionist Edvard Munch, who painted *The Scream* and suffered from mental illness, once said, "I would not cast off my illness, for there is much in my art that I owe to it." The future holds the possibility of correcting genetic faults one day so that fewer fetuses need be aborted. Correcting an inherited disease and avoiding suffering is life-affirming and something that many people would welcome, but enhancing the quality of perfectly healthy embryos smacks of playing God and conjures up the specter of the Frankenstein monster.

Frightening Future

We are becoming familiar with genetic modification in producing cereals, vegetables, and fruits that are more resistant to disease and herbicides, produce heavier and more uniform crops, and have longer shelf lives as a result. How far these developments will go depends as much on the attitudes of consumers as on the creativity of science or the faith of investors in the new products. Ideological battle lines have been drawn between those who delight in progress and those who reject it, whether they believe that "nature knows best" or fear encouraging an invasive and "masculine" technology. Even the Prince of Wales has joined the fray and asked, "[Do] we have the right to experiment with, and commercialize, the building blocks of life?"

Imagine the call to arms when a technological equivalent to the one that gave us transgenic wheat and soybeans is introduced into the marketplace of human reproduction. Imagine a superman or a superwoman engineered from a perfect sperm and a perfect egg and carbon copied as identical clones. Will our increasing ability to control the quality as well as the amount of reproduction in a free and competitive society allow a monster to spring loose? Or will nature always try to preserve variety and refuse to sanction such a triumphal take-over by technology? We cannot deny the powerful drive within us to invest our very best in our children, and apply the benefits of discovery. Reproduction may be a private matter, but how far society will be content to leave the choices up to couples and individuals we have yet to see.

Choosing the Sex of a Baby

Meredith Wadman

Throughout history many parents have wished for the ability to choose the sex of their children. Now, the technology for sex selection has become a reality. In the following article journalist Meredith Wadman describes how the technology works and what ethical implications it raises. A baby's sex is determined by sperm: A sperm bearing an X chromosome will create a female baby, while a sperm bearing a Y chromosome will make a male baby. In humans, the smaller Y chromosome makes the "male" sperm about 2 percent lighter in DNA. MicroSort technology uses this tiny difference to separate the sperm in a sample. The all-male or all-female sperm can then be inserted into an ovulating woman's vagina to fertilize her egg. Wadman reports that the technology primarily has been used to help women carrying the genes for sex-linked genetic diseases, which normally affect boys. Such women can elect to have only girls. However, a wider use of the technology raises ethical issues. Some critics worry that in cultures where boys are preferred, girls will become increasingly rare. Others are concerned that sex selection may be the first step toward the production of designer babies. Meredith Wadman is a freelance writer based in Washington, D.C. She frequently writes on biotechnology and medical issues.

A new technology lets parents order up the sex of their child. It's poised to become big business—and a big ethical dilemma.

Parents have been trying to choose the sex of their children for as long as they've been having them. In ancient Greece, Aristotle counseled men to tie off their left testicle to guarantee a son. The Talmud advises husbands to hold back and let wives take their pleasure first if they want boys. In

Meredith Wadman, "So You Want a Girl?" *Fortune*, February 19, 2001, pp. 174–82.

late-20th-century America, an obstetrician named Landrum B. Shettles built a near-cult following for a best-selling book that advised timing sex to ovulation: several days before if you want a girl, at or near the event for a boy. None of these, nor a thousand other recipes that humans have cooked up over the ages, have been proved scientifically. That's another way of saying that, at least in the eyes of the medical establishment, they just don't work.

The Genetics & IVF Institute, an infertility clinic in Fairfax, Va., has a sex-selection technology that does work. By separating male from female sperm, the process, called MicroSort, gives parents the power to choose the sex of babies before they're conceived, with a high degree of success—especially, so far, with girls. "Finally someone has developed a method of sex selection that is honest and not a fraud," says Sherman Silber, director of the Infertility Center of St. Louis at St. Luke's Hospital and author of *How to Get Pregnant with the New Technology*. "Because everything prior to MicroSort has been clearly in error or frankly fraudulent."

The Virginia institute didn't invent MicroSort; improbable as it may seem, the technology is a creation of the U.S. government. A Department of Agriculture (USDA) scientist invented it in the late '80s as a way to pick the sex of livestock. That nascent business will bring in $100 million a year in the U.S., Europe, and Japan by 2010, estimates XY Inc., the Fort Collins, Colo., company that is developing the technology. But the privately owned Genetics & IVF Institute, founded by maverick entrepreneur-physician Joseph Schulman, holds the exclusive license to apply MicroSort to humans until the government's patent expires in 2009. Without fanfare, the institute has embarked on a gradual but potentially explosive plan to take the choosing of boys and girls out of the realm of wishful thinking and into the world of available science—and lucrative business.

Lack of Regulation

Sex selection is virtually unregulated in the U.S., to the distress of ethicists. That's because Congress has steered almost entirely clear of the hornet's nest of New Age baby making. The Food and Drug Administration (FDA) has the power to pronounce on a machine's safety and effectiveness—the institute says the FDA has approved its sperm-sorting machine—but not on the ethics of how it's used. As for the USDA, it is loath to get in the way of licensees trying to commercialize its inventions. Its technology-transfer program, which generates $2.6 million a year in royalties from 221 licensees, was set up to move government inventions off the shelf and into commercial use. While the USDA theoretically has the power to stop a licensee from sublicensing, it has never exercised that power. So when MicroSort is unleashed in a big way, it will be controlled mainly by market forces—such as the budgets and desires of parents themselves.

MicroSort first made headlines in 1998, when the institute announced it had successfully produced infant girls for 13 of 14 couples in a clinical trial. Since then the institute has delivered 134 more MicroSort babies, with at least 90 more on the way, and it is looking into sublicensing the technology. Meanwhile, because the USDA has patented the technique only in North America, Europe, Australia, and Japan, doctors from countries like India and South Korea (where the cultures strongly prefer boys) are free to pursue the technology now. Some are already doing so. "It's an immense market," concludes Robert Edwards, the British scientist who co-engineered the first test-tube baby.

Institute founder Schulman, 59, a secretive sort who refuses almost all interview requests (including ones for this story), gave up his CEO title in 1998 but still exercises considerable power as the institute's medical director and chairman of its board. He has a long history of pioneering in ethical gray zones. Under Schulman, the 350-employee institute charged several women $11,000 each for removing an ovary and freezing pieces of it before cancer chemotherapy—a method of preserving fertility that had succeeded in only one large animal (a sheep) and that is unproved in humans. The institute also flouts federal law by refusing to report its in-vitro-fertilization success rates to the Centers for Disease Control. Schulman argues that such numbers are meaningless for an individual patient. "Joe thinks he can do anything, pretty much," says a former associate. "And a lot of what he does is motivated by the business of medicine, not the beneficence of medicine." The institute declines comment, but Schulman defender Samuel Marynick, medical director of the Baylor Center for Reproductive Health in Dallas, chalks up such comments to sour grapes. "It's hard to be at the top of the mountain," Marynick says. "People are shooting at you all the time."

Detecting and Sorting Sperm

Ten years ago [in 1991], Schulman and Ed Fugger, a crew-cut Texan reproductive biologist who had developed the institute's huge sperm bank, visited the Beltsville, Md., lab of Lawrence Johnson, a USDA scientist. They knew that the unassuming Johnson, widely considered the world expert on sperm sorting, had spent the previous decade developing an effective sperm-sorting technique for animals.

What Johnson had done—and what the USDA had applied to patent—was adapt a sophisticated cell-sorting machine called a flow cytometer to exploit the fundamental difference between male and female sperm. Male sperm carry a Y chromosome; females an X. The X chromosome holds more DNA—2.8% more in humans and about 4% more in animals. So when sperm stained with a DNA-seeking fluorescent dye are zapped with a laser as they flow through the machine, female sperm, having taken up more dye, glow more brightly.

This difference in brightness allows the cytometer to sort the sperm by sex.

Johnson walked Schulman and Fugger through his lab, where two flow cytometers were sorting bull sperm. More than 100 rabbits, cows, pigs, and sheep had been born using the technique, he told them, and they were all perfectly normal; the dye and laser didn't appear to damage the sperm or the resulting animals.

Schulman and Fugger asked about the possibility of using the technique to sort human sperm. They had a particular group of potential patients in mind: couples who carry genes for rare inherited diseases, such as hemophilia and muscular dystrophy, that occur in boys. (Nearly all sex-linked genetic diseases affect boys, not girls.) These parents could benefit hugely if sperm sorting could be moved successfully from animals to people.

Johnson had tried sorting human sperm, but had hit a daunting obstacle: His machines weren't sensitive enough to check whether sorted samples were, indeed, heavily male or heavily female. (The machines could check animal sperm because the larger 4% DNA difference makes the job far easier.) Schulman and Fugger told Johnson they had good news. They had already refined a lab technique for analyzing chromosomes that would allow them to check the sorted sperm in a petri dish. Huddling in Johnson's small office, poring over machine readouts, the three men hatched a collaboration. Johnson would sort human sperm in his lab; at the institute, scientists would check the sorted sperm for their male and female proportions. Two years later, in a groundbreaking paper in the peer-reviewed medical journal *Human Reproduction*, the men reported that they had successfully sorted human sperm.

In the meantime the institute, with Fugger in charge, moved quickly to launch a sperm-sorting project, buying and adapting a flow cytometer. There was plenty of incentive: Three weeks after the USDA patent was issued, in August 1992, the USDA granted the institute exclusive license to use the technology for the patent's full 17-year term. Such a long license period is standard for the USDA, which reasons that licensees need that much time to make a return on their often considerable investment. (Neither the institute nor the USDA will reveal the licensing fee the institute paid.)

The institute soon launched a trial to demonstrate scientifically that MicroSort was both safe and effective. The trial was approved by the human experimentation review board at nearby Inova Fairfax Hospital, whose parent company, Inova Health System, is part owner of the institute. In the freewheeling world of reproductive medicine, the institute wasn't required by law to seek anyone's approval beyond getting the FDA's nod on its sperm-sorting machine. But it was important to MicroSort's scientific reputation—not to mention its commercial prospects—to be seen as taking the ethical high road.

The hospital board approved the trial only for couples who carried genes for inherited diseases afflicting boys. The first MicroSort baby, a girl, was born in 1995 to a mother who had lost two male fetuses (and three brothers) to so-called X-linked hydrocephalus, a disorder that fatally swells the brain. Since then the clinic has produced daughters for six more couples with disease genes. More girls are on the way: Julie Strasser, 33, an elementary school teacher in Peachtree City, Ga., who carries the gene for Duchenne's muscular dystrophy, is expecting twin daughters in May. Her 30-year-old husband, James, a plastics-plant operations director, calls MicroSort "an answer to our prayers."

As word of the trial spread, says Fugger, his phone began ringing. It wasn't the parents of hemophiliacs who were calling; it was dozens—then hundreds—of couples who, for no medical reason, were eager to choose the sex of their next child.

Surmounting Ethical Barriers

Fugger pondered how he might expand the trial without causing an ethical uproar. His solution was to offer the treatment to parents trying to conceive a child of the sex found in fewer than half of the family's existing children. Unmarried couples, childless couples, and wives over 39 would be excluded. Critics could hardly blast the institute for opening an ethical Pandora's box: MicroSort would be correcting sex ratios, not skewing them. That argument found sympathetic ears at the USDA, which had licensed the method only for use against boy-linked genetic diseases. At the institute's request, officials broadened the license to include any human uses. (A USDA spokesperson refused comment.) A newly constituted institute ethics board also approved the change.

In 1995 the institute began offering the service it calls, delicately, "family balancing." Fugger says he's thrilled that he is not just helping provide the children of parents' dreams, but also helping them avoid the financial strain of having a passel of children before the boy or girl they want appears. "It's just a win-win situation for families who want to use this," he says. Karen and Bill, an upstate New York couple with three young sons, enthusiastically agree. Karen gave birth to daughter Meghan, via MicroSort, [in July 2000]. "My boys are my everything," says Karen, "but I still wanted to experience that mother-daughter bond. Now I'll get that chance to see her go on her first date, be there on her wedding day. I am still on cloud nine!"

While MicroSort is straightforward as science-assisted-baby-making procedures go, it also involves considerable time and money. Couples must submit to a battery of preliminary blood and semen tests. Women often take ovulation-inducing drugs, which insurers may or may not pay for. (They never pay for the sperm sorting.) Couples then must travel to Fairfax, where most women go through several days of ultrasound monitoring before doctors determine that they are ovulating.

On the appointed day, the husband produces a sperm sample in the morning. A machine sorts it, and that afternoon doctors inject the male or female fraction into the wife's womb by catheter—a procedure known as intrauterine insemination, or IUI. The odds of getting pregnant by MicroSort are now 21% a try, the same chance that fertile couples have of getting pregnant the old-fashioned way in any given month. The average MicroSort couple tries three times, at $3,200 a pop, before getting pregnant or dropping out. ([In January 2001] the institute started offering a cheaper $2,300 option for couples who pinpoint the woman's ovulation time themselves, whether by having her own gynecologist monitor her or by using over-the-counter ovulation predictor kits.)

Of the MicroSort babies and current MicroSort pregnancies where the gender has been confirmed, the success rate for conceiving girls is currently higher than that for boys—90% vs. 70%. Among the reasons: X sperm glow more brightly than Ys in the sorting machine, so it's easier to pick them out. The chances of conceiving a boy are climbing steadily, though, as the technology improves. "I would anticipate that ultimately the two would be equal," says USDA scientist Johnson, who recently retired.

International Demand

Despite the drawbacks, the institute continues to field between 250 and 500 calls a month from interested parents, who often must wait several months to enroll. "Yesterday I had a call from Nigeria," said Fugger in late October [2000]. "The day before I had a call from India. Last week I had a call from Germany. They are coming from everywhere." In response to the demand, Fugger has doubled his laboratory staff and is upgrading his three $300,000 sperm-sorting machines so that they can sort a sperm sample in two hours instead of four. He'll soon add another sorter. The changes, he anticipates, should double the lab's capacity. Right now, operating seven days a week, the clinic handles 60 couples a month.

Fugger says that the trial will end after it has demonstrated unequivocally that MicroSort is safe. He estimates that will take as many as 750 babies because genetic abnormalities are so rare in the general population, against which the MicroSort babies have to be compared. The trial has revealed no problems so far, and MicroSort's animal-safety record is spotless.

However, the institute's quest for impeccable safety data in no way limits its freedom to do business, and to sublicense, today. "Literally we could open a site tomorrow anywhere we wanted," says Fugger. "We are developing a strategy to provide access to this to patients not only in the U.S. but in many other countries." He says that MicroSort will probably be available outside Fairfax in three to five years, with providers eventually making profits of 30% or so, but he won't say exactly where.

Some fertility doctors are skeptical about why the institute is taking so long to sublicense MicroSort, wondering if the technology really works. "If you make a claim in a peer-reviewed journal that you can do something that nobody else can, then it's a bit unusual not to be sharing the technology so that others can replicate its efficacy and safety," says Alan Copperman, the director of reproductive endocrinology at Mount Sinai Medical Center in New York City. Fugger responds that the institute hasn't yet sublicensed because of the complexity of the technology, the need for highly trained people to run sperm sorters, and the fact that most of his energy has been focused on the clinical trial.

Of course, outside North America, Europe, Australia, and Japan, anyone can start MicroSorting today, without a sublicense. "It's something that anybody that really knew what they were doing could do," says Sue Sharrow, manager of the flow-cytometry facility at the National Cancer Institute.

If that isn't already happening, it's likely to very soon—and Asia is the most probable place. "The preference for male children is universal in Asia," says Dr. Indira Kapoor, the South Asia regional director at the International Planned Parenthood Federation. According to a December United Nations report, amniocentesis and ultrasonography have made abortion of female fetuses "a booming business" in Asia, especially in India, China, and South Korea. South Korea leads the world in ending girls' lives before they begin—115 boys are born there for every 100 girls.

Moral Concerns

Many would argue that using MicroSort to choose a boy before conception is a better idea than aborting a girl after conception. Still, it is hard to overstate the outrage and indignation that MicroSort prompts in people who spend their lives trying to improve women's lot overseas. Wide availability of MicroSort technology, if it comes, "will be disastrous for society," says Kapoor. "People will go for boys. Girls will not even be conceived."

The technology will certainly be too expensive for most Asian couples, at least initially. But in a population of billions, appealing to a sliver of affluent customers can deliver up hefty profits. So it's not surprising that doctors from India and South Korea, Thailand and Hong Kong are calling the institute, clamoring to know when they can start MicroSorting. Mervyn Jacobson, chairman of Cytomation, a Fort Collins, Colo., manufacturer of animal sperm-sorting machines, says that he's had inquiries from groups in China, Turkey, Taiwan, and Brazil wanting to buy his equipment for human use. When first contacted by *Fortune* in December, Jacobson said the company was preparing to ship a sperm sorter to South Korea for human use this year. The South Korean importer, Jacobson said, is "a very sophisticated professional scientist" in the midst of negotiating a sublicense with the institute. But, says Jacobson, the scientist won't agree to an interview and has since put the deal on hold. The institute declines comment.

Ethical concerns aren't limited to Asia. In surveys, a consistent one-third of Americans say that they have deep moral problems with sex selection—even before conception, and even for families that already have a large number of children of one sex. The objections don't seem to lie in concerns about sexism but in a deep-rooted antipathy to meddling with nature.

U.S. ethicists, meanwhile, worry about the social effects of widespread MicroSorting. Americans have a long-standing preference for first-born sons; will we become a nation of little sisters, conferring selectively on sons the purported advantages of first-borns? (Fugger says that more than half the couples who've approached him want girls.) Will MicroSort children face unforgiving pressure to be just the kind of boy or girl their parents dreamed of? "What happens if you end up having a girl who wants to climb trees and play with mud? Who doesn't have any desire to go to ballet class?" worries Lori Knowles, an associate for law and bioethics at the Hastings Center, a medical ethics think tank in Garrison, N.Y.

Most of all, ethicists fear that a broad embrace of MicroSort would open the door to yet more troubling practices, like jiggering genes to produce designer babies, with everything from hair color to IQ ordered up. MicroSort would "accustom people to getting what they order. A child becomes something that is increasingly a commodity," says Dorothy Wertz, a social scientist at the University of Massachusetts Medical School–Shriver Division in Waltham, Mass.

Worried about being ostracized, most MicroSort patients will not agree to be publicly identified. "Many people who go to MicroSort don't tell others about it. People don't agree with the procedure," a Florida mother of two boys wrote in an e-mail to *Fortune* just before getting in her husband's private plane to fly to the institute. "My husband and I are not telling our friends or family."

Large Market Potential

How big is the potential market? The back-of-the-envelope calculation goes something like this: Each year, some 3.9 million babies are born in the U.S. In surveys, a consistent 25% to 35% of parents and prospective parents say they would use sex selection if it were available. If just 2% of the 25% were to use MicroSort, that's 20,000 customers. If they, like current MicroSort patients, average three tries at getting pregnant at today's $3,200-per-try price tag, that's a $200-million-a-year business in the U.S. alone. "We estimate a U.S. market of between $200 million and $400 million, if (sperm sorting) is aggressively marketed," says Samuel Isaly, an analyst at OrbiMed Advisors, a New York City asset-management group that owns a $50 million stake in Swiss fertility-drug company Serono.

Cost could be the chief obstacle to MicroSort's becoming as common as, say, amniocentesis. "It's expensive enough that the pregnancy rates will have to be very high before MicroSort is widely used by fertile couples," says Richard Scott, director of Reproductive Medicine Associates of New Jersey in Morristown.

But many experts predict that costs will fall. Consider the flow cytometers used for sperm sorting—big, complex instruments that cost up to $500,000 and are designed for dozens of tasks, from diagnosing leukemia to discovering new genes. "If there's enough market, somebody will make a little tiny machine designed only to do (human sperm sorting)," says the National Cancer Institute's Sharrow. That will bring down the price, she says, along with the level of expertise required in operators.

For some, MicroSort may be the stuff of dreams; for others it's more like a nightmare. But for all of us, this technology will soon force intense examination of what we believe about having children, about being parents, about our kids and their place in the world. As Maria Bustillo, a Miami fertility specialist and former institute doctor, puts it: "Just because you want a particular kind of baby, should you have it? Just because you can afford it, should you have it? It's what keeps me awake at night sometimes."

The Prospect of Designer Babies

Lori B. Andrews

In the following selection law professor Lori B. Andrews explores the implications of technologies that will increasingly open the door to prenatal genetic enhancements. Already, corporate researchers have begun to patent genes that would supposedly produce "better" children. In the future, she writes, genetic interventions will make it possible to change the race of a baby or eliminate acne and baldness. What's more, when polled, many parents express a willingness to improve their babies' intelligence through genetic engineering. Such a development would have an enormous effect on society, she contends. Not only would genetic enhancements change the definition of "normal," Andrews argues, it would create new health risks for babies. Lori B. Andrews is director of the Institute for Science, Law, and Technology. She teaches law at the Kent College of Law in Chicago.

Aborting a fetus who is the "wrong" sex and searching for [male] Y-bearing sperm are only the crude first steps in the evolution of designer babies. Soon parents will have more precise tools for genetic engineering.

In vitro fertilization made preimplantation genetic testing possible. The ability to do chromosomal or genetic testing on an embryo led to a further possibility: the chance to treat the embryo when it suffers from a defect or to manipulate its characteristics if by some criterion they don't "measure up."

"It is by bringing the embryo out of the womb and into the light of day that IVF (*in vitro* fertilization) provides access to the genetic material within," Princeton biologist Lee Silver says. "In a very literal sense, IVF allows us to hold the future of our species in our own hands."

The market for genetic enhancements of children is huge—a much more lucrative area for biotech companies to invest in than the treatment of rare genetic disorders. According to a March of Dimes survey, 43 percent of parents would use gene therapy to give their child enhanced physical abilities, and 42 percent of parents would upgrade their child's intelligence level. With over 4 million births in the United States per year, that's a market for genetic enhancement almost as large as that for Prozac or Viagra.

There are approximately 6,000 to 15,000 children in the United States with stunted growth because their pituitary does not produce enough hGH (human growth hormone). Those children are the proper candidates for treatment with a genetically engineered version of hGH. But 20,000 to 25,000 children per year are injected with hGH. Physicians admit that 42 percent of their patients do not have classic growth hormone deficiency; some are just a few inches shorter than average. In a medical research survey, 5 percent of suburban Chicago tenth-grade boys said they had used the hormone.

Human growth hormone has become the forty-third-largest-selling drug in the United States, with nearly a half billion dollars a year paid to the companies that market it, Genentech and Eli Lilly. Even the National Institutes of Health [NIH] has sponsored a twelve-year study, . . . giving human growth hormone to normal, healthy children. Not surprisingly, Eli Lilly has given significant funding to NIH to undertake the study, but it is still costing U.S. taxpayers about $200,000 per child.

The hormone doesn't always work, though. Some kids exceed their expected height by as much as five inches, but others turn out to be shorter than they would have been expected to be without treatment. And according to the American Academy of Pediatrics, there are potential side effects: leukemia, exaggeration of scoliosis, swelling, allergy, and impaired glucose tolerance.

In Charlotte, North Carolina, children were measured at school, and letters were sent to parents suggesting that short kids might need medical attention. Unbeknownst to parents, the nurse running the program was paid $108,000 in consulting fees by Genentech, and her husband was the sole pediatric endocrinologist in the area. One set of parents says the endocrinologist tried to pressure them to try hGH on their eleven-year-old son, who was projected to grow only to five-foot-six. The doctor played on the mother's guilt, asking what she would tell her son when he grew up and learned that he could have been five-foot-ten.

Should society allow doctors to prescribe a potentially dangerous intervention for someone merely because of social prejudice?

Improving the Genes

"Genetic enhancement is going to happen," says W. French Anderson, the nation's leading gene therapy researcher. "Congress is not going to pass a law keeping you from curing baldness."

Various researchers—including Anderson—have patented gene insertion techniques that would let parents insert desirable genes into embryos to create "better" children. University of Chicago physician-philosopher Dr. Leon Kass has speculated that "the new technologies for human engineering may well be the 'transition to a wholly new path of evolution.' They may therefore mark the end of human life as we and all other humans know it." He points out how jaded we've become, quoting Raskolnikov, the protagonist in Fyodor Dostoyevsky's *Crime and Punishment*: "Man gets used to everything—the beast."

Chillingly, one geneticist told me how genetic engineering could be used to cure racism: "We would just make everyone the same race."

Like the parents of Garrison Keillor's fictional Lake Wobegon, most parents want all their children to be "above average." What happens to our definition of *normal* after genetic enhancement hits the scene?

"There will be many wealthy people willing and eager to pay the price of making their child taller and more beautiful," says Michael S. Langan, a vice president of the National Organization for Rare Disorders. "Eventually there will be discrimination against those who look 'different' because their genes were not altered. The absence of ethical restraints means crooked noses and teeth, acne, or baldness, will become the mark of Cain a century from now."

Challenging Normality

Some researchers actually propose putting into people genes from other species, such as a gene to photosynthesize. Scientists have put firefly genes in tobacco plants, causing them to glow in the dark, and human cancer genes in mice, leading to the patented DuPont oncomouse. Law review articles have begun to ask how many human genes were needed before a creature would be a protected person under the Constitution.

I asked my law students what they thought.

"If it walks like a man, quacks like a man, and photosynthesizes like a man, it's a man," said a doctor-turned-lawyer in the class. The very boundaries of what is considered human are being challenged by the technology.

The same is true with cloning. After Jonathan Slack cloned headless frogs, other researchers suggested cloning headless humans to serve as organ donors. They argued that, with no brain, such creatures would not be considered persons under the law.

Limiting Choice

Philosopher Peter Singer and Australian lawmaker Deanne Wells suggest limiting the power of parents to choose their children's traits. They advocate creation of a governmental body to consider parents' proposals for genetic engineering. The body would consider whether the proposed form of genetic engineering would, if widespread, have harmful effects on individuals and society. Part of Singer and Wells's concern is that "if there is pressure on individuals to compete for status and material rewards, the qualities that give children a winning edge in this competition are not necessarily going to be the most socially desirable." The gene for greed might help an individual get ahead on Wall Street, but that might not be the best for the rest of us.

The loss to individuals and society if genetic tampering becomes routine is hardly ever mentioned. Gene therapy to eliminate sickle cell disease is being investigated, even though carrying a single copy of the sickle cell gene is beneficial—it protects against malaria.

At James Watson's Cold Spring Harbor Laboratory, I was part of a conference addressing the provocative question, What if there was a gene that was bad for the individual but good for society? The gene at issue was for manic-depression, a disorder from which many artists and writers have suffered. Some participants at the meeting suggested society would lose out if all manic-depressives were eliminated before birth.

Biologist Lee Silver was not convinced by such an argument. "If the manic-depressive Edgar Allan Poe were never born, we wouldn't miss 'The Raven.' Likewise, we don't miss all of the additional piano concertos that Mozart would have composed if he hadn't died at the age of thirty-four."

The legal and bioethics communities are coming up empty even trying to think of analogies to guide them in this area. Is it "cheating"—akin to taking steroids in sports—for parents to give their kids the genes for height? Or is it more like buying children computers, sending them to soccer camp, or giving them music lessons?

There are medical dangers from gene manipulation, which should give pause to parents who are considering using the technology to upgrade their otherwise healthy kids. When new genetic material is inserted into a cell, it can damage an existing gene, causing it to fail to function. Five percent of mice given gene therapy have such harmful mutations. Should parents and doctors be allowed to take that risk with their children-to-be? And who would "own" the genetically manipulated child?

Drugs from Breast Milk

Researchers from Baylor College of Medicine in Houston have applied to the European patent office for a patent on women who have been genetically engineered to produce pharmaceutical products in their breast milk. So far, the researchers have only used the technique on animals, but they included women in the application, says their lawyer, because of the possibility that whole people may someday be patentable.

Paul Braendli, head of the European patent office, responded with a terse statement: "Human beings are not patentable." But Baylor is appealing, saying human patenting is not explicitly prohibited under European law. Braendli replied that according to the European Patent Convention, patents must not contravene "public order" or "morality."

Interestingly, under U.S. law, there is no such exception. "Anything under the sun that is made by man" is patentable, according to the U.S. Supreme Court, no matter what the impact on society.

Reproductive Cloning

Committee on Science, Engineering, and Public Policy,
National Academy of Sciences

Human embryos have been cloned, but so far as is known no human baby has been born as the result of cloning technology. Nevertheless, cloning has become the focus of intense public interest. In the following selection a panel assembled by the Committee on Science, Engineering, and Public Policy of the National Academy of Sciences and several other institutions explains that a clone is a living entity that has the same genetic makeup as another living being. Cloning typically involves removing the nucleus of an ordinary cell from an adult and placing it into the center of a hollowed-out egg. The process is called somatic cell nuclear transfer. For reproductive purposes, the egg is then implanted in a female's womb. (It can also be placed in a lab dish and coaxed into producing undifferentiated stem cells, a process generally called therapeutic cloning.) The Committee on Science, Engineering, and Public Policy is a joint undertaking of the National Academy of Sciences, the National Academy of Engineering, and the Institute of Medicine. The Panel on Scientific and Medical Aspects of Human Cloning is chaired by Irving L. Weissman, a doctor who serves as a professor of pathology and developmental biology at Stanford University.

Clone is a word that is now commonly used in many contexts in the United States. For example, rather than purchasing a name-brand computer, we might purchase its clone, which provides close to the same benefits but at a lower cost. If we're running out of time, we might say that we wish we had a clone that could help us accomplish all our tasks. When biologists use the word *clone*, they are talking specifically about DNA molecules, cells, or whole plants or animals that have the same genetic makeup.

"Cloning" is achieved commonly in the world of horticulture by, for example, providing a branch or stem of a plant with water and the right environmental conditions and producing a new plant that is a clone, or genetically identical copy, of the original plant. In human reproduction, cloning occurs naturally when identical twins are produced.

Life scientists conducting research today often clone cells to obtain replicas of the bacterial, animal, or plant cells necessary to perform repeated experiments. They can also develop from a single cell large numbers of identical cells (a "clonal cell line") that can be used for experiments and to test new medicines. Scientists clone DNA ("molecular cloning") so that they have large quantities of identical copies of DNA for scientific experiments.

Animal Cloning

Cloning of adult animals, known as reproductive cloning, has become relatively widespread since the report of the birth of Dolly the sheep in 1997; Dolly was the first clone of a mammal produced from an adult cell. Mammals of five species— sheep, mice, pigs, goats, and cattle—have now been successfully cloned from adult or fetal cells, and attempts are being made (so far without success) to clone monkeys, dogs, horses, and other animals in the same way.[1] The cloning of mammals involves a process called nuclear transplantation or somatic cell nuclear transfer (SCNT). In biological terminology, clones are not replicas of each other, but contain identical genetic material.

The nuclear transplantation procedure is also used for a purpose distinctly different from cloning whole mammals. Like reproductive cloning, the process of nuclear transplanta-

1. In August 2005 a South Korean team of researchers reported the first success in cloning a dog.

tion to produce stem cells (also called "therapeutic cloning, nonreproductive cloning, or research cloning") involves placing the DNA from one mammal into an enucleated egg (an egg from which the chromosomes have been removed). Thereafter, the egg is stimulated to divide. At the blastocyst stage of embryonic development (in humans, a 5–7 day old preimplantation embryo of about 150 cells), its inner cell mass is harvested and grown in culture for subsequent derivation of embryonic stem cells. These cells are then used for scientific and clinical investigations. Neither the cells nor the blastocyst are ever implanted in a uterus, as is required for reproductive cloning and the birth of an animal. . . .

Natural and Artificial Clones

Reproductive cloning is defined as the deliberate production of genetically identical individuals. Each newly produced individual is a clone of the original. Monozygotic (identical) twins are natural clones. Clones contain identical sets of genetic material in the nucleus—the compartment that contains the chromosomes—of every cell in their bodies. Thus, cells from two clones have the same DNA and the same genes in their nuclei.

All cells, including eggs, also contain some DNA in the energy-generating "factories" called mitochondria. These structures are in the cytoplasm, the region of a cell outside the nucleus. Mitochondria contain their own DNA and reproduce independently. True clones have identical DNA in both the nuclei and mitochondria, although the term *clones* is also used to refer to individuals that have identical nuclear DNA but different mitochondrial DNA.

Two methods are used to make live-born mammalian clones. Both require implantation of an embryo in a uterus and then a normal period of gestation and birth. However, reproductive human or animal cloning is not defined by the method used to derive the genetically identical embryos suitable for implantation. Techniques not yet developed or described here would nonetheless constitute cloning if they resulted in genetically identical individuals of which at least one were an embryo destined for implantation and birth.

The two methods used for reproductive cloning thus far are as follows:

Cloning using somatic cell nuclear transfer (SCNT). This procedure starts with the removal of the chromosomes from an egg to create an enucleated egg. The chromosomes are replaced with a nucleus taken from a somatic (body) cell of the individual or embryo to be cloned. This cell could be obtained directly from the individual, from cells grown in culture, or from frozen tissue. The egg is then stimulated, and in some cases it starts to divide. If that happens, a series of sequential cell divisions leads to the formation of a blastocyst, or preimplantation embryo. The blastocyst is then transferred to the uterus of an animal. The successful implantation of the blastocyst in a uterus can result in its further development, culminating sometimes in the birth of an animal. This animal will be a clone of the individual that was the donor of the nucleus. Its nuclear DNA has been inherited from only one genetic parent.

The number of times that a given individual can be cloned is limited theoretically only by the number of eggs that can be obtained to accept the somatic cell nuclei and the number of females available to receive developing embryos. If the egg used in this procedure is derived from the same individual that donates the transferred somatic nucleus, the result will be an embryo that receives *all* its genetic material—nuclear and mitochondrial—from a single individual. That will also be true if the egg comes from the nucleus donor's mother, because mitochondria are inherited maternally. Multiple clones might also be produced by transferring identical nuclei to eggs from a single donor. If the somatic cell nucleus and the egg come from different individuals, they will not be identical to the nuclear donor because the clones will have somewhat different mitochondrial genes.

Cloning by embryo splitting. This procedure begins with *in vitro* fertilization (IVF): the union outside the woman's body of a sperm and an egg to generate a zygote. The zygote (from here onwards also called an embryo) divides into two and then four identical cells. At this stage, the cells can be separated and allowed to develop into separate but identical blastocysts, which can then be implanted in a uterus. The limited developmental potential of the cells means that the procedure cannot be repeated, so embryo splitting can yield only two identical mice and probably no more than four identical humans.

The DNA in embryo splitting is contributed by germ cells from two individuals—the mother who contributed the egg and the father who contributed the sperm. Thus, the embryos, like those formed naturally or by standard IVF, have two parents. Their mitochondrial DNA is identical. Because this method of cloning is identical with the natural formation of monozygotic twins and, in rare cases, even quadruplets, it is not discussed in detail in this report.

Clones, Like Twins, Differ

Even if clones are genetically identical with one another, they will not be identical in physical or behavioral characteristics, because DNA is not the only determinant of these characteristics. A pair of clones will experience different environments and nutritional inputs while in the uterus, and they would be expected to be subject to different inputs from their parents, society, and life experience as they grow up. If clones derived from identical nuclear donors and identical mitocondrial donors are born at different times, as is the case when an adult is the donor of the somatic cell nucleus, the environmental and nutritional differences would be expected to be more pronounced than for monozygotic (identical) twins. And even monozygotic twins are not fully identical genetically or epigenetically because mutations, stochastic developmental variations, and varied imprinting effects (parent-specific chemical marks on the DNA) make different contributions to each twin.

Additional differences may occur in clones that do not have identical mitochondria. Such clones arise if one individual contributes the nucleus and another the egg—or if nuclei from a single individual are transferred to eggs from multiple donors. The differences might be expected to show up in parts of the body that have high demands for energy—such as muscle, heart, eye, and brain—or in body systems that use mitochondrial control over cell death to determine cell numbers. . . .

Human Cloning

In principle, those people who might wish to produce children through human reproductive cloning include:

- Infertile couples who wish to have a child that is genetically identical with one of them, or with another nucleus donor

- Other individuals who wish to have a child that is genetically identical with them, or with another nucleus donor

- Parents who have lost a child and wish to have another, genetically identical child

- People who need a transplant (for example, of cord blood) to treat their own or their child's disease and who therefore wish to collect genetically identical tissue from a cloned fetus or newborn.

Possible reasons for undertaking human reproductive cloning have been analyzed according to their degree of justification. For example, it is proposed that human reproductive cloning aimed at establishing a genetic link to a gametically infertile parent would be more justifiable than an attempt by a sexually fertile person aimed at choosing a specific genome.

Transplantable tissue may be available without the need for the birth of a child produced by cloning. For example, embryos produced by *in vitro* fertilization (IVF) can be typed for transplant suitability, and in the future stem cells produced by nuclear transplantation may allow the production of transplantable tissue.

CHAPTER 3

Personal Experiences with Reproductive Technology

Surrogate Mothering Can Lead to Bitter Disputes: The Case of Baby M

Kenneth D. Alpern

Surrogate parenting sometimes results in bitter disputes after the birth of the child. In the following selection Kenneth D. Alpern relates a notable case in which two couples battled in and out of court over a child referred to in court records as Baby M. The couples, Mary Beth and Richard Whitehead, and William and Elizabeth Stern, became embroiled after signing a contract for a surrogate birth. Under the terms of the contract, Mrs. Whitehead was artificially inseminated with sperm from Mr. Stern, and after carrying the resulting baby to term, Mrs. Whitehead was to give her up to the Sterns to raise as their own. However, once Baby M was born, both couples sought permanent custody of her. At one point, the Whiteheads illegally fled with the baby as police sought to turn her over to the Sterns. A trial court granted the Sterns custody and terminated Mrs. Whitehead's parental rights, but the Whiteheads appealed the decision. The New Jersey Supreme Court ruled that the contract amounted to baby selling and therefore violated public policy. The court decided, however, that it was in Baby M's best interests to live with the Sterns, provided that Mary Beth Whitehead retained visitation rights. The parties reluctantly accepted the decision. Alpern observes that the Baby M case illustrates the need for better laws governing surrogacy. Philosopher Kenneth D. Alpern is the George and Arlene Foote Chair in Ethics and director of the Center for the Study of Ethical Issues at Hiram College in Ohio.

In 1985, William Stern, Mary Beth Whitehead, and Richard Whitehead entered into an agreement for surrogate motherhood through the Infertility Center of New York (ICNY), headed by leading surrogacy broker Noel Keane. The agreement was arranged by ICNY, which had recruited Mrs. Whitehead, brought the parties together, provided all the contracts, and in general facilitated the arrangement, for which it received a fee of $7,500. By the terms of the agreement, Mrs. Whitehead would be artificially inseminated with Mr. Stern's sperm, carry a child to term, give up her parental rights to the child, thus allowing Mr. Stern's wife, Elizabeth, to adopt, and receive $10,000 in addition to all costs associated with her pregnancy. On March 27, 1986, Mrs. Whitehead gave birth to a healthy baby girl but decided not to give up the baby.

For nearly two years, the Sterns and the Whiteheads contended for the child, who became famous under her name in legal documents, "Baby M." Early on, the Sterns obtained a court order for temporary custody of the child, but the Whiteheads evaded police, at one point handing the baby out through their bedroom window with the Sterns and authorities in their living room. For three and a half months Mrs. Whitehead hid with the child in various locations in Florida. Finally discovered by detectives, she was forced to give over the child to Mr. Stern's temporary custody while the parties battled in the courts.

Four days after the baby's first birthday, Judge Harvey Sorkow of the New Jersey Superior Court for Bergen County held that the surrogacy contract was valid and enforceable, awarded Mr. Stern permanent custody, and completely terminated all Mrs. Whitehead's parental rights. Judge Sorkow, without giving notice to the Whiteheads, then called the Sterns into his chambers and immediately processed Mrs. Stern's adoption, making her the legal mother of the child.

Appeal by Surrogate

The Whiteheads appealed these decisions, and finally, in February 1988, the New Jersey Supreme Court reversed the lower court's decision on the validity of the contract and, though concurring in the award of custody to Mr. Stern, refused to terminate completely Mary Beth Whitehead's parental rights. She remains the child's legal mother, with weekly visitation rights.

The case of Baby M has commanded national attention, both because of the controversial nature of surrogacy—this being the first surrogacy case to be fully argued in court—and because of the sensational details of this particular case. Spectacular cases can distort underlying issues, but with care, the Baby M case can be used to examine, in concrete detail, many of the moral, legal, and policy issues raised by surrogacy. These issues include whether surrogacy is exploitive of the mother or child; whether surrogacy arrangements must be recognized under constitutional rights to privacy, reproductive freedom, and freedom of contract; and whether regulations should govern any surrogacy practices that are allowed. . . .

Differences Between Families

In public discussion of the case, emotions tended to fix on one or another feature of the parties. The Sterns are well educated, reasonably well-to-do professionals: he is a biochemist, she a medical doctor with a Ph.D. in genetics. The Whiteheads are blue-collar: she dropped out of high school and has been a housewife with a number of menial part-time jobs; he served in Vietnam and drives a sanitation truck. The Whiteheads have suffered through financial problems, a bankruptcy, Richard Whitehead's drinking problem, and a short separation. On the other hand, the Whiteheads have two children, who by all accounts were reasonably well raised and cared for. The Sterns had put off starting a family until they had established their careers and then feared that Elizabeth Stern's recently self-diagnosed multiple sclerosis would make pregnancy too risky for her. Mr. Stern is the last in his family line, most of his relatives having died in the Nazi Holocaust. The Whiteheads had defied the law in absconding with the baby; Mrs. Whitehead was emotional, her appeals were appeals of love and, some claimed, of hysteria. The Sterns were controlled and rational. They had the contract and the legal system on their side. They had used the police to force a mother to give up her child. Mrs. Whitehead had signed a contract and then reneged.

By the time the controversy came to court, two issues had emerged as the most basic legal concerns: the status of the contract and the custody of the child. As to the contract, many felt the simple principle was that when adults knowingly and freely sign a contract, they should do as they said they would. Furthermore, it was argued, constitutional recognition of freedom in matters of reproduction should be understood as extending to the freedom to make and have legal protection of surrogacy arrangements. According to this way of thinking, the terms of the contract settle all issues of custody and parental rights. Less recognized in public debates, however, was the fact that courts have discretion as to what remedy to impose in cases of breached contracts. . . .

Trial Court Decision

The case of Baby M involved two primary court decisions, the initial trial and its appeal, as well as a number of motions and determinations concerning temporary custody and visitation rights. The initial trial was presented before Judge Harvey Sorkow, the judge who had awarded temporary custody to the Sterns at the beginning of legal wrangling over the child. Judge Sorkow's decision surprised virtually everyone by upholding the contract. He further ruled, with somewhat puzzling logic, that the proper enforcement of the contract was specific performance as long as that would be in the child's best interest. He then determined that the child's best interest required precisely what the contract had stipulated: that William Stern have custody and that Mary Beth Whitehead's parental rights, including any right to visitation, be completely terminated. . . .

Judge Sorkow concluded that on all counts the Sterns promised to be better parents for the child than the Whiteheads. The Sterns had planned for the child; the Whiteheads had not. The Sterns both hold graduate degrees, and Mrs. Stern is also a pediatrician; Richard Whitehead was an unenthusiastic high school graduate, Mary Beth Whitehead a high school dropout. The Sterns "have a strong and mutually supportive relationship" and make decisions rationally, with respect and cooperation; the Whiteheads "appear to have a stable marriage now" but have been plagued with separations, domestic violence, problems with alcohol, and severe financial difficulties requiring the family to move their home numerous times. The Whiteheads hardly showed cogent thought in their attempts to evade the law. Furthermore, "Mrs. Whitehead dominates the family . . . [and is] thoroughly enmeshed with Baby M, unable to separate out her own needs from the baby's. . . ." She has been shown to be impulsive (by, among other things, her flight to Florida in violation of a court order), manipulative (threatening, seriously or not, to harm herself and the child), and exploitive (e.g., in her attempts to use the media by exposing her older daughter to the media for sympathy and drawing her into a false charge of sexual abuse against William Stern). Finally, as for helping the child come to grips with her origins, Mrs. Whitehead "has shown little empathy for the Sterns and their role and even less ability to acknowledge the facts surrounding the original contract," and she has shown a propensity to mold facts to her own perceptions. "The Sterns, [on the other hand], have indicated a willingness to obtain professional advice on how and when to tell his daughter" the facts of her origin and have approached all matters rationally, whether routine or in crisis. Thus, Judge Sorkow concluded, "Melissa's best interests will be served by being placed in her father's sole custody."

The Whiteheads' appeal to the Supreme Court of New Jersey, the highest court in the state and a widely respected court throughout the nation, challenged virtually all parts of the lower court's decision. The supreme court consisting of seven members, ruled unanimously [in February 1988] to reverse the lower court in key matters. It invalidated the contract and, though awarding primary custody to William Stern, reinstated Mary Beth Whitehead's parental rights, including visitation. Key parts of the supreme court's decision are as follows.

"We invalidate the surrogacy contract because it conflicts with the law and public policy of this State. While we recognize the depth of the yearning of infertile couples to have their own children, we find the payment of money to a 'surrogate' mother illegal, perhaps criminal, and potentially degrading to women. . . ."

"We find no offense to our present laws where a woman voluntarily and without payment agrees to act as a 'surrogate' mother, provided that she is not subject to a binding agreement to surrender her child. Moreover, our holding today does not preclude the Legislature from altering the current statutory scheme, within constitutional limits, so as to permit surrogacy contracts. Under current law, however, the surrogacy agreement before us is illegal and invalid. . . ."

Conflict with Legislation

Baby-selling. The contract stated and the Sterns contended that money was being paid for services and expenses, but the court had "no doubt whatsoever that the money is being paid to obtain an adoption" (baby-selling), which "is illegal and perhaps criminal." This use of the money is shown by the following: the money was not to be paid until the child had been surrendered, parental rights terminated, and adoption facilitated; no payment was to be made if the child was stillborn before five months, and only $1,000 if later, even though all supposed services would then have been rendered; Mr. Stern was to assume the Whiteheads' expenses in connection with the adoption. In addition, Mr. Stern's contract with ICNY stated that ICNY would coordinate the adoption, and that if Mr. Stern arranged a further pregnancy with Mrs. Whitehead, a further fee must be paid by Mr. Stern—clearly indicating that ICNY arranged not just services but adoptions.

The Supreme Court of New Jersey rejected the lower court's view that surrogacy avoids the evils of baby-selling: "The evils inherent in baby bartering are loathsome for a myriad of reasons. The child is sold without regard for whether the purchasers will be suitable parents. The natural mother does not receive the benefit of counseling and guidance to assist her in making a decision that may affect her for a lifetime. In fact, the monetary incentive to sell her child may, depending on her financial circumstances, make her decision less voluntary. Furthermore, the adoptive [or genetic] parents may not be fully informed of the natural parent's medical history."

"Baby-selling potentially results in the exploitation of all parties involved. Conversely, adoption statutes seek to further humanitarian goals, foremost among them the best interests of the child. The negative consequences of baby buying are potentially present in the surrogacy context, especially the potential for placing and adopting a child without regard to the interest of the child or the natural mother."

Surrender of the child and termination of parental rights. The court noted that the legislature had carefully crafted the law to provide for voluntary surrender of custody of a child only to an approved agency, to make surrender irrevocable only after stringent conditions had been met, including thorough counseling for the natural mother, and to allow surrender only after the birth of the child. Contractual surrender of parental rights is not provided for and agreements to establish paternity are specifically invalidated. The court then judged that these statutory safeguards of the child's well-being are entirely ignored in the surrogate's "contractual concession, in aid of the adoption, that the child's best interests would be served by awarding custody to the natural father and his wife—all of this before she has even conceived, and, in some cases, before she has the slightest idea of what the natural father and adoptive mother are like." The surrogacy contract attempts to circumvent all these carefully crafted institutional protections of the child's well-being and of natural mothers against coercion.

Conflict with Public Policy. Public policy is that children should remain with and be brought up by both natural parents, that deviations from this goal are to be decided on the basis of the best interests of the child, and that the mother and father have equal rights concerning their children. The surrogacy contract, however, guarantees the permanent separation of the child from one of its parents, replaces the child's best interests with an agreement signed in advance, and gives the father exclusive rights to the child. The impact of failure to follow public policy "is nowhere better shown than in the results of this surrogacy contract. A child, instead of starting off its life with as much peace and security as possible, finds itself immediately in a tug-of-war between contending mother and father."

New Jersey's policies call for extensive independent counseling and evaluation in termination and adoption proceedings. In this surrogacy arrangement, in contrast, Mary Beth Whitehead received one hour of legal counseling from an attorney retained for this purpose by ICNY. There is no indication that the psychological counseling she received was for her benefit at all. She was only told that "she had passed." The Sterns relied entirely on ICNY; they were not told that Mary Beth Whitehead had expressed misgivings, and they knew little about her psychological and medical history. The court concluded: "It is apparent that the profit motive got the better of the Infertility Center."

Child's Best Interests

"Worst of all, however, is the contract's total disregard of the best interests of the child." As the court observed, there is no indication of attempts to determine the fitness of the Sterns as parents, their superiority to the Whiteheads, or the effect on the child of not living with her natural mother. "Almost every evil that prompted the prohibition of the payment of money in connection with adoptions exists here." Indeed, continued the court, the payment of money causes *more* problems in surrogacy than in adoption. In adoption, unlike in surrogacy, money is not essential for the process to continue as a social institution; money does not initiate the creation of a child; nor does the child go to the highest bidder. Furthermore, in surrogacy, unlike adoption, "consent occurs so early that no amount of advice would satisfy the potential mother's need, yet the consent is irrevocable" according to the terms of the contract. "[A]ny decision prior to the baby's birth is, in the most important sense, uninformed, and any decision after that [is] compelled by a pre-existing contractual commitment, the threat of a lawsuit, and the inducement of a $10,000 payment. . . ." The surrogate, thus, does not, then, go into the arrangement "with her eyes open"; her need of money is used to take away her child, just as in the more common exchanges of money for adoption. "In the scheme contemplated by the surrogacy contract in this case, a middle man, propelled by profit, promotes the sale. Whatever idealism may have motivated any of the participants, the profit motive predominates, permeates, and ultimately governs the transaction."

Furthermore, the court continued, the surrogate's "consent is irrelevant. There are, in a civilized society, some things that money cannot buy. In America, we decided long ago that merely because conduct purchased by money was 'voluntary' did not mean that it was good or beyond regulation and prohibition [as exemplified in laws concerning child labor, the minimum wage, and equal pay for equal work]. There are, in short, values that society deems more important than granting to wealth whatever it can buy, be it labor, love, or life."

"Beyond that is the potential degradation of some women that may result from this arrangement. In many cases, of course, surrogacy may bring satisfaction, not only to the infertile couple, but to the surrogate mother herself. The fact, however, that many women may not perceive surrogacy negatively but rather see it as an opportunity does not diminish its potential for devastation to other women."

"In sum, the harmful consequences of his surrogacy arrangement appear to us all too palpable. In New Jersey the surrogate mother's agreement to sell her child is void. Its irrevocability infects the entire contract, as does the money that purports to buy it."

Termination of Parental Rights. Though *custody* is to be determined by the best interests of the child, the only ground for *termination* of parental rights is "intentional abandonment or very substantial neglect of parental duties without a reasonable expectation of reversal of that conduct in the future." The court judged that nothing supports such a finding in the case of Mary Beth Whitehead; indeed, the trial court itself had "affirmatively stated that Mary Beth Whitehead had been a good mother to her children. . . . We therefore conclude that the natural mother is entitled to retain her rights as a mother." . . .

Custody. The New Jersey Supreme Court . . . agreed with the lower court that primary custody should be awarded to Mr. Stern. It did, however, go out of its way to comment on what it called the "harsh judgment" of Mrs. Whitehead by the lower court and by some of the experts who testified. Mary Beth Whitehead did break the agreement she had made, and she did wrongly violate a court order even if that order was erroneous, but the court observed, "it is expecting something well beyond normal human capabilities to suggest that this mother should have parted with her newly born infant without a struggle. Other than survival, what stronger force is there? We do not know of, and cannot conceive of, any other case where a perfectly fit mother was expected to surrender her newly born infant, perhaps forever, and was then told she was a bad mother because she did not. We know of no authority suggesting that the moral quality of her act in those circumstances should be judged by referring to a contract made before she became pregnant. . . . We do not find it so clear that her efforts to keep her infant, when measured against the Sterns' effort to take her away, make one, rather than the other, the wrongdoer. The Sterns suffered, but so did she. . . . [H]ow much weight should be given to her nine months of pregnancy, the labor of childbirth, the risk to her life, compared to the payment of money, the anticipation of a child and the donation of sperm?"

The supreme court rejected the view that Mrs. Whitehead's actions during the legal battle showed her to be a selfish, grasping woman ready to sacrifice the interests of her children. It judged rather that the evidence suggested nothing other than a motive of love and that had she been allowed to keep the child, she would have acted unremarkably.

The supreme court did hold the child's educational prospects to be a legitimate concern, but added that "a best-interests test is designed to create not a new member of the intelligentsia but rather a well-integrated person who might reasonably be expected to be happy with life. . . . Stability, love, family happiness, tolerance, and ultimately, support of independence—all rank much higher in predicting future happiness than the likelihood of a college education."

In its final decision to award primary custody to William Stern, the court cited the greater stability of the Stern household and noted that none of the expert witnesses called by the Whiteheads clearly asserted that the Whiteheads' custody would be in the child's best interests, while both of the experts called by the Sterns and, most persuasively, all three experts called by Baby M's court-appointed guardian *ad litem* "unanimously and persuasively recommended custody in the Sterns."

Visitation Granted. The lower court had terminated Mary Beth Whitehead's parental rights and so did not consider the matter of visitation. The New Jersey Supreme Court ordered that this matter be considered but directed that a different trial judge be assigned to the case. The court did stipulate, though, that Mrs. Whitehead was entitled to some sort of visitation, which, given the established relationship between her and the child, would be in both their interests. The court added, finally, that Mrs. Whitehead "is not to be penalized one iota because of the surrogacy contract."

Mary Beth Whitehead's visitation rights were conclusively determined on April 6, 1988, when Judge Birger M. Sween, of the New Jersey Superior Court, granted most of her requests. She was allowed to see the child unsupervised at home, at first for one day a week for up to six hours; after five months a second day would be added every two weeks, and after another seven months an overnight stay would be allowed. In addition, she could be with the child for an uninterrupted two weeks in the summer of 1989, and at certain holidays as well. The Sterns were unhappy that their wish to bar visits until the child was ten years old (unless she asked to see her mother) was not granted, but they elected not to appeal. Judge Sween directed both Mary Beth Whitehead and the Sterns to undergo counseling to help them deal better with their differences. He also prohibited the parties from public discussion of their relationships with the child and urged Mary Beth Whitehead not to call the child by the name "Sara," which she had chosen, but by the name "Melissa," given by the Sterns and recognized by the courts.

The Aftermath

Advocates of surrogacy, including women who had been surrogates themselves, had hailed the trial court's initial decision.

Broker Noel Keane noted that in the period between the two trials his inquiries had quadrupled. Brokers in general pointed to a high rate of satisfaction among the parties to surrogacy, citing a figure of only five or six disputes in over 600 cases. Even after the New Jersey Supreme Court's reversal, brokers claimed that surrogacy would continue to flourish, especially in states that did not follow the New Jersey Supreme Court's lead. Indeed, few brokers had *ever* thought that surrogacy contracts were enforceable. The Sterns' lawyer, though, said he would counsel his clients against surrogacy as too legally precarious.

Many opponents of surrogacy had rallied around Mary Beth Whitehead during the first trial. Just before the first decision, a group of 135 prominent American women circulated an open letter under the title "By These Standards, We Are All Unfit," asserting that virtually no one's character could withstand the hostile scrutiny Mary Beth Whitehead had received. The same unsympathetic attitudes with which Judge Sorkow and the press approached the Whiteheads could also have painted an ugly portrait of the Sterns. The point here is not to claim that the Sterns are terrible people or that they will be less than good parents. Rather, the point is that biases of class and gender seriously prejudice judgments about this case and about surrogacy generally. Mary Beth Whitehead breached a contract, absconded with her child, and generally expressed her emotions openly. These actions occasioned outrage, and her character was vilified in the press, in popular understanding, and by a superior court judge. Yet disputes over contracts, even those involving children, rarely occasion *outrage*. Defenders of Mary Beth Whitehead pointed out that the odd behavior in these circumstances would be the ability to sublimate one's emotions. Not until after the New Jersey Supreme Court decision was there much of an attempt to imagine sympathetically what it must be like to have the police appear without notice at one's door with a court order to remove one's newborn child. It was a major breakthrough for the supreme court to finally recognize officially that Mary Beth Whitehead is *not* a surrogate mother or "surrogate uterus," but rather the natural, biological mother of the child.

In light of such observations, some commentators charged that appeals to violation of the contract and the court order were merely rationalizations for popular sentiment against Mary Beth Whitehead, and that the deeper motivation for such feelings was indignation that a blue-collar housewife got out of line and was so presumptuous as to fight by whatever means she could find against the structures of power and status—of money, lawyers, contracts, and courts—that were aligned against her.

The decision by the New Jersey Supreme Court clearly calls out for legislation explicitly addressed to surrogacy. Though the court condemns commercial surrogacy, its decision leaves it open for the legislature to create new laws allowing surrogacy under various guises. The court does, however, seek to instruct by showing that the rationale for close state regulation of adoption—to protect the interests of children, mothers, and the state adoption—also applies to the surrogacy situation.

As for this particular case, the outcome of the arrangement for the individuals directly involved is that none of the adults got what they wanted. The Sterns did not get a child to raise in privacy and in the illusion that the child is related to no one but themselves. Mary Beth Whitehead failed to find the fulfillment of providing a loving gift to others, and she refused the monetary compensation to which she was entitled. Noel Keane, the broker, received his fee and notoriety that may perversely have increased his business, but in the longer run the legal climate may have shifted significantly against surrogacy. And Melissa Stern, who had no representative in the formulation of all the agreements, has lived through two years of disruption and instability. If we *hope* that she will now be able to grow up and live her life in peace and security, we must also *act* to create regulations and practices to ensure that children and parents in the future will not have to suffer as they have in this case.

Three Women Donate Eggs to Their Sisters

Alanna Winter and Judith C. Daniluk

Egg donation is a difficult experience for women. It requires numerous blood tests, the use of specialized and sometimes hazardous drugs, and a surgical procedure to retrieve the eggs when they are ready. In the following selection two experts in counseling and reproduction issues relate the experiences of three women who donated eggs to their sisters. In their study Alanna Winter and Judith C. Daniluk interviewed the women after their sisters gave birth in order to gain insights into the psychological dimensions of their act. To protect the subjects' privacy, the researchers assigned the women pseudonyms. "JR," "Mary," and "Lola" all reported that the donation process was trying but ultimately rewarding. Despite difficulties along the way, all three appear to be profoundly gratified that they were able to help their sisters become mothers. Alanna Winter counsels at the Elizabeth Bagshaw Women's Clinic and Planned Parenthood in British Columbia, Canada. Judith C. Daniluk is a professor of counseling psychology at the University of British Columbia.

During in-depth interviews, 3 women whose egg donations resulted in the birth of a child or children for their sisters discussed their donation motivations and decisions, the challenges of the donation procedure, and their postdonation feelings and experiences in the years since the birth of their nieces and nephews. The findings of this narrative study support the viability and advantages of this form of family building and highlight the counseling and support needs of known donors throughout the process. . . .

Alanna Winter and Judith C. Daniluk, "A Gift from the Heart: The Experiences of Women Whose Egg Donations Helped Their Sisters Become Mothers," *Journal of Counseling and Development*, vol. 82, October 1, 2004, pp. 483–95. Reproduced by permission. No further reproduction authorized without written permission from the American Counseling Association.

Unlike sperm donation, egg donation is physically arduous and time-consuming. The donor must have repeated blood tests and ultrasounds, daily injections of powerful fertility drugs, frequent medical monitoring, and an invasive medical procedure to retrieve her eggs when they are ready to be fertilized. The medications and the retrieval process are associated with some risk. In light of this fact, it is not surprising that, historically, the practice of egg donation began with the donations of friends, family members, or acquaintances known to the recipient couple. Familial donations are the most common form of known donation and are often preferred by infertile women because of their shared genetic and familial history with the donor. . . .

The Donors

Four women from a Vancouver fertility clinic, whose egg donations had resulted in the birth of a child or children for their sisters, had agreed, subsequent to their donation, to be contacted for follow-up research. These women were sent a letter from the clinic explaining the nature and purpose of the study and requesting their participation. Three of the women agreed to participate in the study. One donor declined because she was concerned that her participation would violate her commitment to her sister to maintain complete privacy regarding her donation. Consistent with the demographic profile of known donors described in the literature, . . . the three participants were well-educated, middle-class, Caucasian women who were married and had their own children. The first participant . . . was 37 years old and had two children. The son born to her sister from this woman's donation was 2 years old. The second participant was 35 years old and the mother of two children. Her donation helped her sister conceive and carry twins, a boy and a girl, aged 2 years at the time of the interview. The third participant was 36 years old and the mother of four children. The daughter born to her sister as a result of her donation was 3 years old at the time of the study.

Prior to their donation and in preparation for becoming egg donors, each woman and her husband had participated in a mandated counseling session of approximately 90 minutes. The session was both informative/educative and therapeutic and was conducted by a doctoral-level counselor who had several years of experience working with infertile clients within a medical treatment setting. During this session, participants were fully informed of the time commitment that would be required, possible side effects of the medications, potential short- and long-term risks associated with the egg donation procedure, and the parameters of their legal rights. Issues related to expectations, obligations, maintaining appropriate boundaries, disclosure, and privacy were also explored with participants and their partners, and any concerns regarding these issues on the part of the donor or her husband were worked through to the point of resolution and consensus. These issues were also addressed with the recipient couple in a subsequent counseling session. All donor and recipient couples were invited to return for counseling in the future should any issues arise related to their donation experiences. At the time of the research, none of the participants had sought further counseling related to their donation experiences. . . .

JR's Story

JR was 35 years old when she donated eggs to her 38-year-old sister. Describing their relationship as "very close," JR said: "She's the one I call in times of joy and in times of sorrow." After years of watching her sister struggle with infertility drugs and procedures, JR volunteered to help by donating her eggs. She told her sister: "I'd even go so far as to be a surrogate mother if you can't carry a child, so talk it over with your husband and let me know when you're ready to begin." An unexpected miscarriage that occurred after this offer was made only deepened JR's empathy for her sister's plight. After almost a year of contemplation and soulsearching, her sister and brother-in-law accepted JR's offer. Despite some initial concerns regarding the procedure and how JR might feel about the child if treatment was successful, JR's partner put his full support behind the donation. However, for JR, the issue of maternal legitimacy was never a real concern. Her sister would be carrying and giving birth to the baby, which for JR meant her sister would be the mother. JR perceived the genetic and social history she shared with her sister as a tremendous benefit for any child produced through her "gift of love."

The medical and counseling orientations were viewed by JR and her partner as "very helpful preparation" regarding the medical, emotional, and social aspects of the donation. JR was surprised by the counseling session in that it "simplified things for her instead of making them more complicated." JR's family members had been told and were "very supportive" of her donation decision, and during the counseling session her sister and brother-in-law resolved that they would also tell the members of his family as well as the child, if treatment was successful. As for possible medical risks, JR felt that "the benefits or end results far outweigh the supposed risks," but she also committed to "only doing it once."

JR found the injections and medications somewhat of a challenge, especially given that these were increased significantly when her eggs did not respond well to stimulation. Having been completely optimistic, it was at this point that the reality that treatment might not work finally hit JR. In her words, "at no point had doubt ever entered my mind and then all of a sudden I thought, oh my god what if it doesn't work?" Rather than sharing her fears with her sister, she used humor to mask her concerns. Fortunately, the retrieval went well, yielding nine eggs, four of which fertilized. Two were transferred to her sister's uterus, and after several weeks of nervousness on "everyone's part" a pregnancy was confirmed by ultrasound. When her sister had successfully completed the first trimester, JR was finally able to enjoy sharing her own pregnancy stories and experiences with her and was there to help her get settled at home when she returned from the hospital after the baby was born.

JR recalled feelings of joy and amazement when her tiny 5'4" sister gave birth to a 9 lb 6 oz boy! She remembered wondering, "Will he look like me?" and acknowledges that even now she still has similar thoughts once in a while when she sees her nephew. She immediately felt and feels a special bond with this child and is certain that this bond will likely always be there—a bond she believes is not at all the same as the one she has with her own children. Rather, it is a bond that comes from knowing she was part of helping her nephew come into this world. Both she and her husband enjoy watching her sister with her son—apparently "they're inseparable."

A Deepening Relationship

Living with the fact that the egg she donated to her sister has resulted in a child has been largely positive for JR. In the 2 years since her nephew was born, JR's relationship with her sister has deepened. JR receives regular updates on her nephew's growth and development, and the children of the two sisters are quite close. Although she and her brother-in-law have always gotten along well, she thinks they are also closer now in terms of being more open and comfortable in their communications with each other. JR and her sister's family members also share a sense of wonder about the fact that JR's donation helped her sister become a mother. As for disclosure, all of the people JR has told were first cleared by her sister. In almost all of the cases, their reactions were positive. "They were excited, they thought it was great," JR related. JR's sister and brother-in-law, as well as JR and her husband, plan to tell their respective children the story of their nephew's conception. When JR's sister tells her son how he was conceived, JR prays he comes through it with a very positive attitude. She hopes he understands that his life is the result of the love she has for his mother and is able to be "matter of fact about his origins." Even if his reaction is not as positive as she hopes, she believes that disclosure is for the best: "It's a far better way to do it than to not tell him. That seems like it's something wrong and it's not."

As far as remaining challenges, JR still struggles with the fact that she would like to help her sister and brother-in-law have another child, but they have not imposed on her in this regard, because it was not a part of their original agreement. Her husband is also not comfortable with JR donating her eggs again, largely because of the toll the donation itself took on their own family in terms of time and resources. Other than these worries, JR does not "anticipate any hardships or problems" in the future as a result of her donation. JR does not expect the close relationship she has with her sister to change as a result of their donation experience.

"We're very close. As kids we were always close, even though there was that age difference. We're the types that will talk on the phone everyday, sometimes twice a day. I feel we can tell each other anything, the first thing I do when I have a situation where I need some advice and I want to talk to someone, I just pick up the phone and call her . . . in times of joy and times of sorrow. We'll just go on the way we are, which has always been close."

In assessing her overall experience of being an egg donor, JR says that donating her eggs to her sister has enhanced her life. She is "just so thankful that I was able to give her the ability to have a child. It's a pretty giving act, and I feel like it's the least I could do for the love that she has shown me her whole life. It's not that I'm repaying her, but a gift that I could give to her. So it feels really good." JR concluded, "We were very lucky it all turned out, and the support we had from our family and the relationship we have. . . . If I didn't have that kind of relationship, I don't think that I would have offered to have done it in the first place." Her sister and brother-in-law are, in her words, "fabulous parents," and she says she is "proud to know that she had a small part in making their dream" a reality.

Mary's Story

Mary volunteered to donate her eggs to her younger sister after watching her make the painful decision to terminate two pregnancies because of serious fetal abnormalities. Mary did not think it was fair that she had two children of her own, and her sister would not have any, so she vowed to help if she could. She discussed the possibility with her husband, whose consent and support were critical to her. For her part, Mary recalled feeling "110% sure" this was the right thing to do. She talked about how the "joy of being a mother" was an important part of her life and said that this was "something she wanted her sister to be able to experience" as well. Although initially reluctant, after researching the procedure more thoroughly, her sister and brother-in-law accepted Mary's offer. The two couples agreed to keep the procedure as private as possible, limiting disclosure to Mary and to her sister's parents and her brother-in-law's parents. Both sets of parents were grateful that Mary would do this for her sister and brother-in-law.

Once the medical procedure began, Mary realized that she was frightened of the risk of ovarian cancer, of the chance that it wouldn't work, and, if treatment was successful, that the child produced from her donation might "end up looking like [her]." Compounding this was her fear of needles and the requirement that she inject medications into her stomach every day for a month. In an attempt to make the experience as positive as possible for her sister, Mary said she elected not to share her feelings or fears with her sister: "Knowing that I had two children of my own is basically what got me through."

Failed Attempt

Mary's sister did become pregnant from the treatment, but miscarried in her first trimester. Mary recalled feeling devastated: "It was like someone had taken a knife and stabbed me in the heart." She said she felt as though she had "failed her sister and brother-in-law," was angry that it did not work, and immediately resolved to do it again: "When something doesn't work for me, no matter what it is, I go into it the second time around not 100% but like 150%." With the support of her husband, Mary said she again endured the difficult procedure. Her sister became pregnant with twins.

Mary was "elated" about her sister's pregnancy and "relieved" when the first 12 weeks passed without any difficulties. However, although she recalled being happy for her sister, the medications required for two cycles of egg donation had taken a tremendous toll on her physically and emotionally—eventually requiring antidepressants to help her cope with her erratic mood swings: "I couldn't stand my emotions, I couldn't control them, and having to take another drug, an antidepressant to control me, the thought of that, I didn't like that either." Realizing that she was "not a pleasant person to be around" and not wanting to breach her agreement about keeping the donation completely confidential, Mary said she withdrew from her family and friends. She did not want to "ruin her sister's happiness," so she withdrew from her as well, although they spoke regularly on the telephone during the pregnancy. Mary recalled this as a very difficult time and said it was by far the "worst part of her donation experience."

Upon reflection, Mary said she realized that her emotional instability during that time was also compounded by her fears about whether her sister would be able to carry the pregnancy to term. Given her commitment to secrecy about her role in the twins' creation, Mary also said she was really concerned about what might happen if one of the babies looked like her: "Every day I was sweating bullets as she got closer to her due date—what are these children going to look like, are they going to look like me?" Although uncertain about how she would feel when the babies were born, Mary said she found the experience of "seeing them for the first time quite moving. . . . In spite of my earlier fears I did really well. I think what it was, was seeing the joy in my brother-in-law. . . . He was just walking on air, and when I saw my niece and nephew, that fear was replaced by joy." She also felt "moved and honored" when, as a tribute to Mary, her sister and brother-in-law elected to give their daughter the name Mary would have chosen for her own little girl had she given birth to a daughter.

During the first 6 months after the twins were born, Mary tried to stay back and out of her sister's way so that she had time to bond with her babies: "I didn't want her thinking that I felt like I should be mothering them." She did not have any maternal feelings toward the babies when they were born and still does not have these feelings 2 years later: "I don't feel like I'm their mom, because I didn't carry them for 9 months and I didn't birth them." Both Mary and her husband find that they often look to see who the children resemble, but Mary is not bothered by that: "It's just all family, it's all blood, and that's just the way I look at it now." Mary does acknowledge that the twins feel "a little extra special" to her.

In terms of the future, Mary admits there are some things that worry her about living with the fact she donated her eggs to help her sister have the twins. The first is the concern for her own health, particularly of getting ovarian cancer. The second is about disclosure. The decision about who should be told—including the twins, Mary's children, friends, and other family members—is not one that Mary takes lightly: "It has to be agreed between the four of us—my spouse, my sister, and her spouse." However, she is fairly confident that they will be able to work things out together: "We know there's a fine line and we know not to step over it. I can't see there being any problems."

Mary says she has felt closer to both her sister and brother-in-law since the donation and the birth of the twins. She describes their relationships as much deeper:

We're just closer, there's a different kind of bond. I figure it'll just be pretty much the same, we'll just keep continuing getting closer. I can't see any problems . . . my brother-in-law is an absolutely super person. No, I just think we'll stay close like we are, if not become even closer. I don't know if we can get closer, I just think we'll have that strong bond between us.

Although the donation experience had its challenges, Mary said she would not hesitate to do it all over if she had the chance to go back. She feels a lot of pride for what she was able to do:

You can buy people a lot of gifts, material gifts, but nothing is more rewarding than what I was able to do—give my sister a part of me so she could enjoy her life and bear children. The joys of actually feeling a child grow and move and kick inside of you, and then giving birth to it, and then watching that little one grow.

That was what she wanted for her sister and that is what she feels she has been able to help her achieve.

Lola's Story

Lola described her donation of eggs to her sister, who was 9 years older, as "a wonderful adventure." She recalled how important being a mother was to her sister and the emotional toll it took on her during the many years she had tried, unsuccessfully, to have children. "I didn't understand why it was so easy for me and my other sister to get pregnant. What was going wrong for her?" Although they lived in different cities, Lola said she and her sister were "very close" and "shared all the joys and trials" of their lives through regular phone calls. When it was confirmed that ovum donation was her sister's only option to produce a child, Lola insisted that with four children of her own, she was definitely finished with her own family and would be delighted to help her sister in any way possible.

After learning more about the procedure, Lola gained an appreciation for the potential disruption this might cause in her life and in the lives of her family members. She wondered, "With the fluctuations of mood and all of that, how would that affect my job and my work and my parenting and my relationship with my husband?" Lola discussed the procedure at length with her husband and received his full support. She also told her four daughters about her decision to donate her eggs to their aunt. She believed that this was a wonderful gift and saw no reason to hide it.

However, Lola's sister was uncomfortable with being open about their plans, and she became quite distressed when, against her sister's wishes and on the basis of her need "to be open and honest," Lola told their mother about the upcoming donation. Despite their mother's positive reaction to the donation, Lola's sister was extremely upset by Lola's disclosure. Consequently, during their predonation counseling session, both sisters worked through and resolved their different feelings and needs regarding disclosure. During the counseling session, issues of privacy and confidentiality were addressed. Lola, who had an extremely close relationship with her mother, explained to her sister why she felt their mother's approval was so important to her prior to going ahead with the donation. Her sister had the opportunity to share her feelings of having her trust "betrayed," and together they came to an agreement as to under what circumstances information about the donation would be shared in the future and with whom.

Lola's only concerns about the donation were related to "the long-term side effects—risks for ovarian cancer and things like that." She had many talks with her friends about the issue of how she would feel about a child that resulted from the donation and felt confident that she could keep the boundaries between herself and the child or children clear.

She believed that she had considered all of the issues involved and felt in her heart that she would feel the same way toward her sister's child as she did toward all her nieces and nephews. As a very spiritual person, Lola said, "I just felt deep within myself a whole peace about it."

Hardships of Donation

For Lola, the actual medical procedure was both trying and rewarding. She gained weight and had hot flashes, pain, and some moodiness. She also had to be away from home for a few weeks because the clinic was located in another city: "It was uncomfortable and put everybody out." Alternately, the experience "brought a lot of people together." She felt well supported by the different people in her life. It was important to her that everything was open and that the whole family shared in this experience, including her children, who were kept informed of what was happening throughout the process.

The retrieval yielded seven eggs, three of which fertilized. Two were good enough to be transferred to her sister's uterus. Although disappointed in the small number of embryos, Lola was also relieved that her sister and brother-in-law would not be faced with decisions they were "very uncomfortable with," such as selective reduction or the destruction of extra embryos.

Throughout the process, Lola said she felt really close to her sister: "I felt like we were on some kind of weird and wonderful adventure. We were doing something together most sisters never get to do. I just felt very privileged to be able to help her in this way." When her sister's pregnancy was confirmed, Lola recalled being thrilled: "I thought, 'this is such a wonderful thing, that people have got to know. This is an amazing miracle that's happening.'" Lola remembers it as one of the most thrilling days of her life when she heard her sister had a beautiful, healthy daughter. Shortly after the birth, she flew in to see her sister and her new niece. Although she said she instantly loved the baby when she first saw her, she was pleased that she had "no maternal feelings" toward the child. She felt amazement that the procedure worked and that this "perfect little girl" was created, but her feelings were clear: "I felt toward her just like I did with my other sister's little girl when she first had her baby."

"Total, Pure Joy"

When asked about her donation, Lola described a sense of "Total, pure joy. I'm amazed and grateful, in awe, so proud of my sister and her husband, proud of my family for supporting me the way they did, just grateful that I'm the one that could have that opportunity." Lola believes that through this special process her relationship with her sister has been enhanced. To highlight this point, Lola talked about how things were between her sister and herself after the birth of the child. "She kept saying 'thank you' and I kept saying thank you to her. It was like bringing our relationship to a whole different level, and a whole different place that nobody else goes to . . . and I also felt that my brother-in-law was a part of that." Lola also feels that the experience has had many positive effects on her other important relationships—especially with her mother, her husband, and her daughters. She says the experience has enriched their lives and family and credits her husband's unwavering support and love in helping her get through the rough spots: "His support confirmed how much he loved me."

Watching her niece grow up has been exciting for Lola. Although she discussed with her daughters that genetically the child is their half sister, she has been sure to emphasize their social bond as cousins. Her sister has kept a photo album and journal of their experience conceiving their daughter and plans to give it to her when they tell her about her origins. It pleases Lola that her sister and brother-in-law plan to tell their daughter about her origins, not only because she dislikes secrets, but because "It makes a beautiful part of her story and

I think she needs to know that she was created by people that love her and that she was so wanted that everybody was willing to do what they could to help." Lola is optimistic about her niece's future development and is looking forward to having the opportunity, one day, to tell her how much she loved her mom and dad and wanted so badly to help them. She believes that openness and honesty are the key ingredients to her positive egg donation experience: "I really feel that it wasn't anything great that I did. I think what we were a part of was really a miracle. I feel grateful that we have this story to tell her, grateful that it happened."

Importance of Support

The findings of this study have the potential to add considerably to an understanding of the counseling needs of known donors at each stage of the donation process. The experiences of these known donors challenge many of the concerns and assumptions expressed in the literature regarding the potentially problematic nature of this form of family building. Their stories also strongly reinforce the importance of thorough predonation preparation and ongoing support in ensuring that the needs of all members of the donation experience—the donor and her family, the recipient and her partner, and the child or children conceived through this process—are taken into consideration at all stages of the donation process.

When Divorce Collides with Surrogacy: The Case of Tessa

David Grogan and Beth Austin

The following selection relates the story of Tessa, a young girl born to a surrogate mother on behalf of a couple who later divorced. Born in 1985 to social worker Lee Stotski, Tessa was claimed by Beverly Seymour and Richard Reams, a married couple who had contracted with Stotski to act as their surrogate. However, the couple failed to file adoption papers, and a year later they went to court to divorce. Each of the divorcing spouses sought custody of Tessa. Complicating matters, a test showed that Reams was not Tessa's biological father, and Stotski, the surrogate mother, also demanded custody of the child. The judge in the case urged both would-be adoptive parents and the birth mother to abandon their fight and let the child be placed with an adoptive family. The judge reasoned that the four-year-old child's interests would be best served by a fresh start. At the time this account was published, courts were continuing to struggle with the unusual case. Since then, developments have taken an even more tragic turn. In 1990 a court awarded Richard Reams custody of Tessa. Shortly afterward, his ex-wife, Beverly Seymour, shot and killed him. She later confessed to the slaying. A jury convicted her of voluntary manslaughter, and she was sentenced to prison. The fate of Tessa is yet unknown. David Grogan and Beth Austin are staff writers for People *magazine.*

Tessa looks just like any other pixieish blond 4-year-old. Her dimpled grin is disarming, and the twinkle in her deep brown eyes hints at a mischievous spirit. She prances as she walks, constantly attended by her trusted teddy bear and stuffed dinosaur. In the presence of strangers she is friendly if not entirely sure of herself. That insecurity disappears, though, when Tessa speaks of her future. "I don't want to grow up," she says. "I want to stay little."

Small wonder. At her tender age, Tessa has already sampled the complexities of the adult world, and she evidently finds them exceedingly strange. The child of a surrogate-parenting arrangement gone tragically awry, Tessa is trapped in a legal labyrinth from which there is no easy exit. Her life is circumscribed by court rulings and crowded with lawyers and angry adults. Even the simple joy of learning to write her own name has been compromised largely because the grown-ups on whom she relies cannot agree on what her surname should be.

Confusion over Parents

Biologically, Tessa is the child of Lee Stotski, a Columbus, Ohio, social worker who gave birth to her on Jan. 21, 1985. The baby was given to Beverly Seymour and Richard Reams, the married couple who had hired Stotski as a surrogate mother. But when their marriage foundered a year later, Seymour and Reams both wanted custody of Tessa. That might have seemed like trouble enough for one baby, but things only got worse. For reasons neither can now adequately explain, Reams and Seymour had failed to file adoption papers. By doing so, they left Tessa in legal limbo.

As the months dragged on, other complications arose. Court-ordered blood tests disclosed that Reams could not have fathered Tessa. Her biological father turned out to be Leslie Miner, a friend of Stotski's who agreed to be a sperm donor after repeated attempts at artificial insemination using Reams's sperm had failed. Miner has since signed away any paternal rights.

For now, Tessa divides her time between Reams's home in Sunbury, Ohio, and Seymour's in Ashville, Ohio, traveling 50 miles twice a week. Stotski, who is also seeking custody of Tessa, sees the child only occasionally. The battle over permanent custody has dragged on for more than two years and required the ministrations of more than a dozen lawyers. Last month [January 1989] the case reached a temporary stalemate in Franklin County Probate Court in Columbus when Judge Richard Metcalf dismissed separate petitions for adoption by Reams and Seymour after they failed to post bonds of $3,000 each to cover the cost of legal representation for Tessa. Metcalf rejected pleas of financial hardship by Reams, whose business failed, and Seymour, who owns a small quilt-and-craft shop. Instead he suggested that Reams and Seymour give up their claims to Tessa and allow her to be adopted by an unidentified East Coast couple reported to have a six-figure annual income. "I started to cry," says Kim Halliburton, the former lawyer for Reams. (Reams has declined to speak to the press.) "I said, 'No, I can't make my client accept that.'" Seymour was equally outraged. "The judge concentrated on how much these people could give Tessa," she says. "I feel like I'm in a bidding war over this kid, and I am the low bidder."

Judge's View

Judge Metcalf doesn't see it that way. "It's our position that we have to seek out the best possible adoption for the child," he says. "In this case we have two people petitioning for adoption who are unrelated to the child and who have divorced. That never makes a happy group. Whereas we could put the child with people who have nothing but pluses." For Metcalf the overriding issue in the case seems to be the continued acrimony between Reams and Seymour. "At some point [Tessa] has to be affected by all the emotional strain," he says. "Those little minds do a lot of thinking. It's too bad adults tear kids up this way."

In the absence of a clear-cut statute concerning surrogate motherhood in Ohio, the legal wrangling over Tessa's future was recently transferred to another venue, juvenile court. There, Reams and Seymour will have to contend with each other and also with Stotski, the birth mother, who has concluded that Tessa would be better off living permanently with her. "I had talked myself into thinking, 'This is not your child. You have no right to tell them what to do,'" says Stotski. "But then I felt guilty about having brought a child into the world and put her into this situation."

Confronted with the array of petitioners all seeking custody of one little girl—Reams, Seymour, Stotski and the unnamed couple back East—some of the lawyers involved are nonplussed. "We find ourselves tongue-tied just trying to decide the players," says Charles Milless, an attorney appointed by the courts to represent Tessa. "And every time somebody turns around, one of the parties files in a new court or changes attorneys." King Solomon would have wept.

When Beverly Seymour and Richard Reams married in December 1979, raising a family was uppermost in their minds. "I tried every means to get pregnant," says Seymour. "I went to several fertility specialists, and everything looked okay." Reams, who sold furnaces and portable kerosene heaters for a living, had a checkup that showed a normal sperm count. Finally, after three years of frustration, Seymour underwent exploratory surgery and discovered that one of her fallopian tubes was blocked, and that it was unlikely she would be able to conceive a child.

In vain Seymour and Reams investigated the possibility of adoption. Then, in 1982, they saw a news story about Kathryn Wyckoff, a Columbus woman who was launching a surrogate-motherhood service. Neither a doctor nor a lawyer. Wyckoff's primary qualification was that she had once been a surrogate mother herself. Seymour and Reams became her first customers.

The Surrogacy

Wyckoff, who charged $3,000 for her services, put the couple in touch with Stotski, who agreed to bear Reams's child for $10,000 plus medical expenses. Married and the mother of three teenage children Stotski imagined herself sharing the joy of parenting with a childless couple. "Everything about the Reamses' marital situation was presented to me as very, very perfect," Stoski says. "The message I got was, 'We want a child. We want to have a family.'"

Three times a month, for six months, Stotski unsuccessfully underwent artificial insemination with Reams's sperm at the office of a Columbus physician. There is disagreement about what happened next. Stotski and Seymour say that Wyckoff suggested using another sperm donor; Wyckoff denies this. Seymour insists her husband agreed. "Nothing was pulled over his eyes," she says. Yet Reams continued to give his own sperm samples to Stotski, and Halliburton, one of his attorneys, says he knew nothing of another donor. The eventual disclosure that he could not be Tessa's biological father "was big news to Dick," Halliburton says.

In the middle of all this, Wyckoff moved to California to start another surrogate service. At that point, Stotski asked Leslie Miner, a 62-year-old co-worker, to be an artificial insemination donor. "He did it as a favor." Stotski says. "He was somebody I trusted and somebody who had dark hair and eyes like Reams."

Finally, after 18 months of trying, Stotski became pregnant. By then Stotski and Seymour had become close friends. "I was there when the amniocentesis was done," says Seymour. "I bought her maternity clothes." Throughout the pregnancy, Stotski kept reminding herself that she could not keep the child. But when she handed the newborn Tessa over to Reams and Seymour, she felt the pull of powerful feelings. "It was much harder than I thought it would be, and I cried for days," Stotski recalls.

When Tessa was born, Stotski had been paid just $1,000 of her $10,000 fee. At the time, she was content with the knowledge that she would be able to see the little girl occasionally and that she had brought immense happiness to Tessa's new family. "We would meet for lunch. We would go to the park," Stotski says. "We all got along fine. They accepted the fact that I wasn't going to take Tessa away. And I accepted the fact that she was well taken care of." Meanwhile, Reams's business was failing, and strains were beginning to appear in their marriage. "Every once in a while Beverly would say she was concerned about money," Stotski recalls.

By March 1985 Reams and Seymour were in deep financial trouble. Seymour says that Reams and his mother, Annabelle, who were in business together, both lost their homes following bankruptcy proceedings. That forced his mother to move into the two-bedroom home that Reams and Seymour shared. According to Seymour, Annabelle soon insisted that the three find something larger. Her presence did nothing to ease the couple's marital problems. "Richard wanted me to work full-time," complains Seymour, "while his mother took care of my child."

Reams and his mother moved out in March 1986, leaving Tessa with Seymour. Four months later, says Seymour, Reams scraped together enough money to pay off the remainder of Stotski's $10,000 fee. Unaware that Reams and Seymour were having troubles, Stotski signed paternity papers identifying Reams as Tessa's natural father. Seymour claims that Reams "used that legal advantage to come to my home anytime he wanted" and once used violence to get his way. "He physically tried to take the child," she says. "He beat up on me pretty bad." Reams vehemently denies that he ever hit his wife.

In June 1986 Reams was able to obtain a court order giving him custody of Tessa, and sheriff's deputies arrived on Seymour's doorstep to take the child from her. "When they came and took her, I just about died," says Seymour. "I didn't see her again for 57 days. I called and begged, but [Reams] would not let me lay eyes on her." In desperation Seymour begged Stotski to intercede. "She said, 'Please, please help me. He won't let me see Tessa,'" Stotski recalls. Sympathetic, she agreed to petition the courts to void Reams's paternity. "That was my mistake," says Stotski. "I should not have gotten involved." It was then that Seymour announced that Reams was not the baby's biological father. "I said, 'This is a fraud,'" she recalls.

In May 1987 Seymour filed for divorce and vowed to fight for custody of Tessa. Once in the case, Stotski found it impossible to extract herself. When blood tests showed that Miner was probably Tessa's natural father, Stotski began to reconsider her own responsibility to the child. She decided that Tessa's life with Reams and Seymour was too chaotic and soon afterward filed for custody herself. "It just didn't seem like Tessa was leading a very good life," she says.

Continuing Conflicts

On a wall in Stotski's two-story home hangs a plaque showing a baby's tiny fist grasping an adult's finger. Dressed in a white blouse trimmed with lace, her blond hair pulled back in a ponytail, Lee Stotski calmly insists she will continue to press for custody of Tessa, with her husband, Joseph, an electrician. "I've always tried to put God's will first," she says. "But I wish I knew what His will is. I just can't figure it out." She and Seymour are no longer in contact, but Reams did invite Stotski to spend some time with Tessa last Christmas. "I gave her this crazy stuffed brown horse with white stockings and the strangest eyes I've ever seen," says Stotski. "I've always loved stuffed animals, and I guess she does too. She doesn't like dolls, and I never did either."

Some 30 miles away, late on a Sunday afternoon, Beverly Seymour is at home with Tessa. Showing a visitor around her modest apartment, Seymour complains that she has had to sell off pieces of furniture to pay her legal expenses. "What I was able to keep after the divorce, I've hocked," she says. But despite the hardship, she maintains, Tessa has been nourished with motherly love. "She has known nothing but lullabies and organic food and homemade dresses," Seymour says, watching Tessa make bright crayon drawings of monsters. "This child was originally conceived for me. From the time Mrs. Stotski got pregnant, I've felt this is my baby. I'm Mommy here." Reciting the litany of her maternal travails, Seymour suddenly breaks down in tears and Tessa races to her side, crying in sympathy. "I'm fine, honey, I'm fine," says Seymour. As Tessa returns to her drawing, Seymour whispers, "She feels what I'm feeling, so I try to be cheerful."

Aware that she is due to spend the evening with the Reamses, an hour away, Tessa repeatedly reminds Seymour, "It's time to go up north, Mommy. It's time to go up north." She seems to find nothing unusual about traveling from one parent to another every few days, and she apparently finds equal pleasure in being with both of them. They, in turn, clearly adore her. "I've seen how Tessa looks at Dick," says Kim Halliburton. "The sun rises and sets in that little girl for him."

If Seymour, Reams and Stotski were willing to set aside their differences for Tessa's sake, they might work out a custody agreement. "If the court felt [a settlement] served the child's best interest, that exists as a legal possibility," says attorney Milless. "As a practical matter, no such agreement seems forthcoming." As biological mother, Stotski would normally have the strongest legal case for custody. But her original decision to allow Reams and Seymour to raise Tessa may be considered child abandonment, cause to deny her any parental rights. All parties consider joint custody between Reams and Seymour unlikely because of the animosity between the two. Whatever their faults, however, Reams and Seymour are the only parents Tessa has ever known. "She's not an infant. She's not oblivious to what goes on," says Halliburton. "These are Mommy and Daddy. And for a small child, that's all the world she's got."

Artificial Insemination for Single and Lesbian Women

Lasanda Kurukulasuriya

Artificial insemination is widely used by infertile couples, but there are others who seek to make use of it as well. In the following selection Lasanda Kurukulasuriya examines the experiences of several single heterosexual women and lesbian couples in Canada who have used artificial insemination. Susan Cole and Leslie Chud, one of the lesbian couples profiled, are the parents of Molly, born to Chud through artificial insemination. As the author relates, they were able to enroll Molly in a day care where the fact that she has two mothers was warmly accepted. The children of other such couples are not so fortunate. Classmates often tease them for having two mothers, Kurukulasuriya reports. All the same, a growing number of women without male partners are opting to become mothers through artificial insemination. Kurukulasuriya profiles several other lesbians who have become mothers through artificial insemination. Such developments challenge the image of the traditional family, but no evidence indicates that lesbians differ significantly from other mothers. Heterosexual women seeking artificial insemination without male partners face fewer problems, as society has grown accustomed to families headed by single parents, the author explains. Lasanda Kurukulasuriya is a freelance writer and a dual citizen of Canada and Sri Lanka. She resides in Sri Lanka.

When Susan and Leslie started sending Molly to day care, other two- and three-year-olds thought she was the luckiest person in the world.

"I mean, what could be better than to have two mothers? All their favorite people are the mothers, you know!" says Susan.

Susan Cole, senior editor at *Now* magazine, is the non-biological parent of six-year-old Molly, born to her partner Leslie Chud, who became pregnant through artificial insemination. Leslie and Susan are among a growing number of women without male partners who are using this procedure to have children.

"It's really something women can do . . . very much part of controlling our reproduction," says Susan. "I certainly learned . . . that this was something you did not have to invite the state into, or invite the medical profession into at all."

Artificial insemination (AI) has been carried out in clinical settings in Canada for 45 years for women whose partners have low sperm-count or absence of sperm. However, the demand for AI services by women without male partners is a relatively recent phenomenon. The majority of fertility clinics across Canada still discriminate on the basis of sexual orientation and family status.

Lesbians Excluded

Out of 33 AI programs surveyed by the Canadian Royal Commission on New Reproductive Technologies (RCNRT), 20 would exclude single women, and 19 would refuse lesbians, the commission's 1993 report reveals.

Over the past two decades a few women without male partners, but wanting children, have begun to take matters into their own hands. They have sought out a male friend, or a friend of a friend, or a relative who was willing to donate sperm, and inseminated themselves, using a (needle-less) syringe purchased from a drugstore.

"This is not a complicated procedure. It's not mysterious . . . to my way of thinking, it's not even a technology," says Susan.

Women have been using AI outside of clinical settings from at least the mid 1970s onwards in Britain and the United States, and from at least the late 1970s in Canada.

It hasn't taken long for self-insemination (SI) to become synonymous with the now-proverbial turkey baster. The reluctance of the medical establishment, generally, to accept unmarried women as recipients of AI on the one hand, and the simplicity of SI on the other, seem to have made it an obvious choice for lesbians who wanted to form families in the late 1970s and 1980s.

Single heterosexual women too, are beginning to see AI as a reproductive option that frees them of the need for involvement with men, as mates or co-parents, or both.

Cathy is a single woman who had her baby with the assistance of a Toronto clinic. She says she would probably have married and had a family if she had met a man she wanted to spend her life with. Having very much wanted a child, from the age of about 25 she had begun to think of AI as a last resort.

Cathy lives with her mother and has a secure government job. She carefully considered her options—adoption, asking a male friend to be a sperm donor before choosing to be inseminated at a clinic. Her daughter Megan is two years old.

A Revolutionary Choice

The fact that women are seeking to have children by AI through choice, not sheer necessity, has revolutionary implications. The decision of a lesbian or single heterosexual woman who uses AI is more visible than that of a woman who has no other option than to use AI with donor sperm owing to her male partner's infertility.

For a woman trying to form a family in the context of a heterosexual relationship, the inability to have a child with genetic links to both parents is usually a cause of grief. The situation of a woman without a male partner is not comparable; she makes no secret of her project.

But for the most part AI's increasing popularity among women without male partners has gone unnoticed, partly owing to the monopolization of the procedure by medical practitioners, and partly owing to popular misconceptions as to what AI is.

Even the use of AI with donor sperm in a clinical setting, by women whose male partner is infertile, is being subjected to public debate only now, under the general rubric of new reproductive technologies (NRTs). It is curious that this should be so, seeing that AI is neither new (the first recorded artificial insemination of a woman took place in 1793) nor a very high-tech procedure. . . .

Up to now, AI has taken place and been discussed mostly in a context of "treating infertility in heterosexual couples," because this is the context in which physicians approve of its use.

But as the RCNRT report points out, "There is in fact no greater medical need in a woman whose partner has no sperm than in a woman who has no partner."

AI is generally described, quite inaccurately, as a "treatment for male infertility." It is not a treatment (in the sense of a cure) and the recipient of the procedure is not a male. The continued use of the term "therapeutic donor insemination" perpetuates this confusion. "Therapeutic" means "curative" or "pertaining to healing" and in fact no attempt is made to cure the male's infertility with AI.

The risk of contracting a disease such as AIDS is a major concern for women trying AI, since the human immunodeficiency virus believed to cause it can be transmitted through semen.

"We started to do this just at the time of the AIDS crisis," says Susan. "There was no way we were going into a clinic at that time. . . . We wanted everybody tested, tested, tested. . . ."

Donation from a Brother

It was Susan's brother who finally became the donor for Leslie's baby. A biological link was thus created between the child and both women's families. Susan says her parents, who were initially a bit surprised at her decision to parent, "had a different stake in it once they found out who the donor was."

While health concerns and the desire to protect themselves from donor claims led Susan and Leslie to choose a known donor, the very same concerns are leading prospective AI recipients increasingly to seek the services of clinics, where they expect that sperm obtained from sperm banks, which use anonymous donors, would be screened for AIDS and other sexually transmitted diseases.

Suzanne Desaulniers, who operates a business from her home in Ottawa, began making inquiries about AI five years ago. She picked up a book from the local women's bookstore. She visited Planned Parenthood. She talked to friends.

"My partner and I discussed the matter, we discussed possible male candidates," says Suzanne, a lesbian. "We had concerns regarding HIV and hepatitis. Could we trust the guy if he said the test proved negative? . . . The biggest issue for us if we used a known donor (was) would he come back and claim access to the child? So we finally decided to use a clinic."

Suzanne discovered that neither the Ottawa Civic Hospital nor the General Hospital would inseminate women without male partners. She went to the only clinic in the area that was open to her—that of Dr. Norman Barwin, a gynaecologist in private practice.

Suzanne's daughter is now almost three. "We have a very happy family. We've just bought a house. My daughter is doing really well," she says. . . .

Desire for Motherhood

The reasons why lesbians and single heterosexual women want to have babies are not very different from those of other people. "I always wanted to have a child" is a recurring response.

There is a difference in their attitude, though, in that they do not see the realization of their desire as necessarily involving male participation. Suzanne explains it like this: "For many years I've wanted to have a child. I was always interested in the whole experience of childbirth. Also, I like children. After my first boyfriend ... I realized that marriage wouldn't suit me."

"Having a child seemed very separate to me. In my early 20s it occurred to me that you don't have to get married to have a child. ... Certainly, I've been able to separate 'the heterosexual family' from having children."

Feminist politics and analysis have given women the "permission and the confidence," to use one woman's phrase, to carry out decisions that two decades ago would have been unheard of.

Margo, an Ottawa woman who has a two-year-old as a result of AI, says the idea that she could have a baby without a husband or boyfriend certainly came from her feminist analysis. (Margo did not want her real name used for reasons of privacy.)

"Some people feel it's one thing to be gay or lesbian and another to raise a child," says Margo, who is a lesbian. "So for sure my political analysis helps, in that the issues around battering and incest make me quite aware that there's no such thing as a 'normal nuclear family.' ... So it allows me to come back to people, to say 'Yes, this will be a different situation, but ... in a sense it's safe and loving, and that's what's important, and a lot of what appears to be the normal family is in fact quite dysfunctional.'"

Of course, people do ask questions like "how can you raise a child without a male influence?" says Margo. Not all women see their decision in feminist terms. "I look at it just as a natural, maternal thing that I want to do. I never thought of relating it to feminism," says Donna Tuck, a single lesbian considering AI. She moved from Toronto to Ottawa mainly to be in an environment she felt would be better for raising a child.

Donna is receptive to the idea of having a known sperm donor who would share parenting. "If I asked a man . . . it would be because it's somebody I respect enough that I would want them to be co-parenting," she says. . . .

If Susan and Leslie have been able to provide a friendly environment for six-year-old Molly to grow up in, it's partly thanks to their privileged social situation which gives them access to good support systems. Molly's day care, for example, was founded 20 years ago by Leslie, who is a social worker associated with developing child-care in shelters for assaulted women. It had an environment that Susan describes as "totally open." They knew the staff many of whom were gay.

Molly was envied by other kids in day care for having two mothers. But her case may not be representative. It would appear that AI children run an emotional gauntlet between public attitudes. Children can be taunted by school-mates who say, "you can't have two mothers; everybody has a mom and a dad."

Single Mothers

The AI children of single women are probably less exposed to stigmatization outside the home than those of lesbian couples, since single parenthood is nothing new or unusual. One fifth of Canadian families raising children are headed by single parents, most of whom are women.

Most AI mothers make it a point to keep in touch with families like their own, so that their children can get to know others in similar situations. They are open with their children and explain, or plan to explain, their manner of conception to them as soon as they seek the information.

There is no evidence to suggest that lesbians are remarkably different than other parents, says Robert Glossop, director of programs and research at the Vanier Institute of the Family in Ottawa.

"I think you would find as much variation in the parenting styles of gays and lesbians as you would find across the range of parenting styles of heterosexual people. So I don't think you can make generalizations."

A lone-parent too, can be an effective parent, he says. "A child needs to know that there's an adult who's absolutely devoted and committed to his or her well-being. The child also needs to know that there's predictability and stability in his or her life."

"A single parent can provide that. It's sometimes more difficult, sometimes more challenging, sometimes more exhausting, more time-consuming, but once again, there's nothing inherent . . . that makes the lone parent a less effective parent." . . .

Changing Family Structures

The image of the traditional family with a male breadwinner, a wife who is not in the work force and two or three dependent children, is not one that is applicable today. Out of the 7.5 million families in Canada, only 3 million are two-parent families raising children under the age of 18, according to a 1991 report of the Vanier Institute of the Family. "There is no longer one typical family in Canada," it says.

It is difficult to imagine how those who want to save the traditional family would impose a model of "appropriate" family behavior, when the people it supposedly benefits are departing from it in droves, in spite of the many institutional underpinnings straining to keep it in place.

Smaller Families

Studies indicate that families are very important to Canadians, and that they continue to be a significant feature of their lifestyle, but that the family forms in which people choose to live have changed tremendously, along with changes in the economy and social mores over the past two decades.

Statistics Canada reports that during this time families have grown smaller, the number of lone parent families has doubled, numbers living in a common-law arrangement have more than doubled, marriage rates have decreased and divorce rates have increased.

The major problem with the concept is not the noun "family," but the article "the," writes sociologist Margrit Eichler, in her book *Families in Canada Today: Recent Changes and their Policy Consequences.* "As soon as we put forward a conception that there is such a thing as 'the family', we are by implication ruling out other similar kinds of groupings as non-family."

Reproductive decisions have never been entirely private, experts say. At all times and in all cultures, they have been controlled by various social rules and proscriptions.

As Susan McDaniel, a sociologist at the University of Alberta writes, "issues related to reproduction and reproductive control, far from being private, are among the most politically contentious of our times."

Which is to say, in a sense, that a humble turkey baster can take us a long way from the kitchen table.

A Grandmother Bears Her Daughter's Children

Lynda Beck Fenwick

In the following selection Lynda Beck Fenwick tells the story of Christa, a young woman who was born without a womb. When the defect was discovered, Christa's mother, Arlette Schweitzer, offered to have her uterus transplanted into her daughter. However, such an operation was not feasible, so Schweitzer settled for the next best thing: At the age of forty-two, she agreed to become impregnated with her daughter's eggs, which had been fertilized in vitro by her son-in-law's sperm. In October 1991, Schweitzer delivered a healthy boy and girl. In doing so, she became the first woman to give birth to her own grandchildren. Far from feeling strange about this, Schweitzer explains that she was simply helping her daughter, as any mother might do. Lynda Beck Fenwick, a former trial attorney, is the author of two books concerning public policy.

When Christa was told at age fifteen that she had been born without a uterus, she and her mother devised a plan. Although it had never been done, they decided that when the time came for Christa to have a baby, her mother, Arlette, would carry Christa's baby for her. Over the years, they held to their plan, believing the technology would catch up with their dream. When Arlette Schweitzer finally became the first American grandmother to give birth to her own grandbabies, people were amazed, but she does not see herself or the surrogacy itself as particularly remarkable. "I was just a mother helping her daughter. It was more like donating a kidney," she says.

In fact, her first offer had been to donate her uterus for transplanting into Christa, but doctors told them this could not be done. Although Christa was born without a uterus, she has ovaries and they produce healthy eggs.

"We had read that there was a test-tube baby born in England, so we thought of doing this. We were aware that it had never been done, and I guess we knew that our chances weren't really good. But I am the kind of person that puts the cart before the horse," Arlette admits. "I just expect things to work out. Even when the odds are against me, I expect them to turn out the way I want."

Among the few people with whom they shared their plan were husband and father Dan and several other members of their close-knit family. Dan supported the idea, but the rest of the family did not take their plan too seriously. "I don't think anyone ever believed we really would do it. Christa, Danny, and I all had the impression over the years that they all felt it was just something we were saying to make ourselves feel better."

Certainly the most important person to join in their plan was Kevin Uchytil, the man Christa eventually married. Christa told him about what she and her mother planned to do very early in their relationship, even before she and Kevin became seriously involved, and he was pleased about the possibility it offered. When Kevin and Christa finally married, they quickly decided to start their family.

As a Catholic, Arlette knew that the Church opposes surrogate births, and although she was committed to carrying Christa's baby, she admits to having struggled with her conscience. "I knew that I wasn't going to change my mind, but I prayed about it and put it in the Lord's hands. From the beginning, Christa and I believed the Lord would decide what He wanted for us, and if it didn't work, we would know it wasn't His will. We both have a strong commitment to Mary, and we also prayed to her."

Because of her respect and affection for their local priest, she never spoke to him about her decision. "I knew his position would have to be one of following the Church, and our position had to be one of following our hearts. I didn't want him to have to be torn."

Dr. William R. Phipps of the University of Minnesota performed the in vitro fertilization and implantation. Eggs were taken from twenty-two-year-old Christa and fertilized with Kevin's sperm before being transferred into Arlette's body. Biologically, the parents and grandmother are exactly as they would have been if Christa had been able to carry her own babies.

Four embryos were transferred, and Arlette explains, "Dr. Phipps warned us about the possibility of all four embryos implanting and told us that some people choose to abort one or two if that happens. We told him right off that whatever the Lord gave us we would accept." Arlette was warned that carrying four fetuses could be risky to her, but because both she and Christa are opposed to abortion, they were determined not to consider it. Only two of the embryos implanted, and within days Arlette had her first ultrasound. "If ever in my life I've thought about abortion, it was on that table at that moment—not thought about having it done—thought about how wrong it was. Because, there I am with these minute grains of rice, less than that, and we're seeing their hearts beating. It was the most profound, profound moment."

Although Arlette's pregnancy was considered high-risk because of her age (forty-two) and her health (asthma), and Arlette was already menopausal by then, physically the pregnancy felt no different to her than when she carried her own children two decades earlier. She acknowledges, however, "With this pregnancy, more than with my own, not only was I a little wiser but the world is a little wiser. We know so much more about the development of these babies. I tried to do everything right—not just the medical aspects but eating right and not taking a drink." She also felt that she had been entrusted with something that was not her own. "It's like comparing caring for your own children with caring for someone else's children. You feel this huge responsibility if something were to happen. I felt that greater responsibility."

Unlike most surrogacy arrangements, Arlette and Christa had nothing in writing. Arlette believes, "It was unwritten because it didn't have to be [written]. We know each other so well, and that is one of the benefits of not hiring a surrogate. Christa knew that I would do everything in my power to have healthy children for her. And I knew that no matter what, she would take these babies, even if they were born deformed or retarded. We went to all the medical examinations together, and I think that if anything would have cropped up, we would have dealt with it the best at that time."

On October 12, 1991, five weeks early, Chad Daniel was born to his grandmother by cesarean section, weighing six pounds and three ounces and measuring 20 1/4 inches long. One minute later, Chelsea Arlette was born, weighing four pounds seven ounces and measuring 18 inches long. On their birth certificates, Kevin and Christa Uchytil are listed as the parents, based upon the sworn statement of Dr. Phipps. Despite their early arrival, both of the twins were healthy, with mature lungs.

Although the family had tried to avoid publicity, a few weeks before the births, news had somehow leaked to the press. With the arrival of the twins, headlines across the nation declared, GRANDMOTHER GIVES BIRTH TO TWINS AS SURROGATE FOR HER DAUGHTER. When Arlette left the hospital five days later, she allowed pictures, but declined to answer any questions except to say she felt fine.

While Arlette would have preferred no publicity, her typically positive attitude has allowed her to find some good in it. "We did not ask for the publicity. It was thrust upon us, but in some instances we can see the benefits of it. Christa has

Rokinpansky-Kuster-Houser syndrome, and we have been contacted by people with this syndrome from as far away as Spain."

We know little about Rokinpansky's, and it occurs in only about one in every five thousand women. Since no woman with Rokinpansky's has ever been able to carry her own child, no one knows whether the syndrome would be passed by the mother to her female offspring. One of the interesting medical benefits of this surrogacy is that for the first time the biological daughter of a woman with Rokinpansky's syndrome has been born, and doctors may learn from Chelsea whether the condition is passed genetically.

As far as publicity about her role as a surrogate goes, Arlette is a very reluctant spokesperson. "I don't even consider myself a surrogate. I was just a mother helping her daughter, and I would never have considered doing it under other circumstances." Since the birth of the twins, she has talked to many other couples considering surrogacy, and she sympathizes. "I understand the need, the desire to want to have a child so desperately." She also recognizes that her own family has benefited from the technology. "I sound so hypocritical, like I am turning things for my own use, but I feel we must be careful of how we use medical technology." Christa is equally certain that had her mother been unable to carry the twins, there would have been no surrogacy. For both of them, the process was a matter of family love and not based upon whatever was technologically possible.

Arlette expresses two particular concerns about surrogacy. First, she doubts whether a hired surrogate shares the same level of responsibility toward the fetus that is felt by a surrogate acting out of love and without compensation for the gestation. "I am not an advocate for surrogacy generally, and yet I am an advocate for someone that would do it because they cared about that other woman—for a sister, a mother, or mother-in-law, or even a very close friend who says, 'I care about you and I know that you need this help.'" She explains further, "A hired surrogate is going to get her money whether she delivers a four-pound, premature baby that hasn't been nourished correctly or whether she does everything exactly as she was supposed to. There's not as much at stake. They are just hired to do a job."

Her second concern involves the use of genetic material from someone other than the couple. Christa's ability to produce the eggs from which Chad and Chelsea were conceived was essential to their plan, and neither Arlette nor her daughter would have considered a surrogate birth using donated egg or sperm. "I think we are playing games with ourselves when we start borrowing the actual makings of the baby from other people and then saying this is my child. I think those are the cases where there are going to be problems."

A surrogate who gestates an embryo created from the egg and sperm of the parents for whom she carries the child normally has no genetic link to the baby. Arlette is different because she has the genetic link of a grandmother whose traits passed through her daughter's egg. As far as she is concerned, her love for Chad and Chelsea is no different from the love she feels for her other three grandchildren, although she admits that she worried a little before they were born about whether there might be a difference. "It's even strange to me. I cannot believe that there is absolutely no difference. I walk into a room, and whichever grandchild gets to me first gets scooped up first." As she struggles to explain how this could be, she remembers something. "It's like when you are expecting your second child. You worry, I love my first child so much that I can't possibly love this second one as much. And then the second one is born and ah! it all just fits into place and you love them both the same. That's the way it is with the grandchildren."

After the birth of Chad and Chelsea, Dan Schweitzer described his new grandbabies as "two little miracles." Grandmother Arlette agrees. "There is no way that anyone could look at Chad and Chelsea and not know that they certainly are a gift from Him." But then she adds, "Just as each child is."

Today the twins are happy, healthy six-year-olds, and Christa and Kevin are relishing their roles as parents. "Motherhood was Christa's vocation," Arlette believes, "and Chelsea is already just like her mom, trying to mother Chad all the time." Christa has decided not to have Chelsea tested for Rokinpansky's syndrome until she is older, but Arlette confides, "I am taking very good care of myself." For a moment the meaning of her comment isn't clear, until she continues: "I don't know if Chelsea will need me—and we all hope she won't—but if she has inherited Rokinpansky's syndrome and wants me to carry her babies for her, too, I will if my health allows it." Arlette is prepared for the skeptical reactions of people to her notion of a great-grandmother surrogate. After all, she and Christa faced years of skepticism. She mentions the possibility of being a surrogate for Chelsea in a casual way, but her sincerity is apparent. "What else could I do if she asked me? I could never deprive her of children and Christa of grandchildren if it were in my power to make it happen."

SCIENCE AND
MEDICAL
DISCOVERIES

CHAPTER 4

Contemporary Controversies over Reproductive Technologies

166

Reproductive Technologies Are Immoral

Bob Smietana

The development of various reproductive technologies—most notable, in vitro fertilization (IVF)—involves the destruction of embryos. In the following selection evangelical journalist Bob Smietana explores the views of Christians who object to such practices on moral grounds. The controversy, he explains, centers on differing views about when "personhood" begins. At one end of the spectrum are those who regard capabilities, such as the capacity for conscious thought or sensation, as the baseline for personhood. At the other end are those who believe that personhood begins at conception. The latter is a view widely held among opponents of technologies that destroy embryos. However, Smietana points out that Christians hold a range of opinions on the question of personhood. Indeed, the growth of IVF has made some evangelicals more flexible in their thinking about the moral status of embryos. Nevertheless, many theologians firmly oppose IVF, Smietana reports. One theologian explains that IVF, in her view, undermines the value of life. Other theologians argue that as humans are made in the image of God, destroying embryos is demeaning to God. Bob Smietana is a features editor for the evangelical publication the Covenant Companion *and a frequent contributor to* Christianity Today.

When Aaron Barg was three months old, a hernia left him in almost constant pain. Finding a surgeon who could repair the hernia was easy, say his parents, Steve and Susan Barg. But finding an anesthesiologist was almost impossible.

With a rare genetic disorder called Trisomy 13, Aaron was born with a weakened heart and lungs and an undeveloped

Bob Smietana, "Where Does Personhood Begin?" *Christianity Today*, vol. 48, July 2004, pp. 24–28. Copyright © 2004 by *Christianity Today*. Reproduced by permission of the author.

brain, and he was deaf and legally blind. Doctors told the Bargs that Aaron would most likely die within a year. If he survived beyond that time frame, his life would have little quality—he'd never speak, walk, or feed himself.

For most anesthesiologists, the risk was too high. They felt any operation could kill Aaron.

Getting the medical community to regard Aaron as a person worth saving was a challenge. Susan Barg remembers that doctors didn't refer to him by name, but only "baby Barg." Though doctors commonly refer to even healthy babies this way, she found it symbolic of their attitude toward Aaron.

"He has a name," she would insist. "Please use it."

During a medical visit, Barg asked an anesthesiologist if he would like to hold Aaron. He did so for a full hour, and only then did he agree to assist in an operation. Since then, the anesthesiologist has helped in several more operations for Aaron.

"He holds Aaron, and he becomes a human being," Barg says. "Not a statistic, not a piece of medical research on a piece of paper, but a human being with a name who responds to touch and cuddling and love."

Now 13, Aaron is a handsome boy with blond hair and a face that lights up when someone he knows comes by. Bend down by his wheelchair and he'll pull your face close to his, stare deeply into your eyes, and stroke your face. Though he can't speak, his eyes and hands tell you that he knows you are there. And he has far exceeded all expectations—he can move his wheelchair, feed himself, and even communicate using five hand signals.

Range of Views on Personhood

Aaron's experience raises hard questions about personhood. There is no scientific agreement over when human life begins, much less when that life attains personhood—or moral standing, personal stature, or a soul.

But the question of personhood, with its incumbent legal and moral implications, is at the nub of all bioethics debates. Do our capabilities make us persons? If that's the case, then some, like bioethics professor Peter Singer of Princeton University, would argue that Aaron is not a person.

If Aaron is not regarded as a person, how much less so the 400,000 human embryos, each the size of the head of a pin, stored in cylinders filled with liquid nitrogen at more than 430 fertility clinics in the United States. What status do they have?

In a recent article on Salon.com, Michael West, CEO of Advanced Cell Technology, a private company working on stem cells, described an embryo as neither human life nor a person, "just an ordinary group of cells."

"It's not a developing human being," West told Salon.com. "There are no body cells of any kind. . . . There are not even any cells that have begun to become any body cells of any kind."

Few in the evangelical orbit would agree with such a statement, but a limited range of belief about personhood does exist among Christians.

Most evangelicals would agree that personhood begins at conception, says John Kilner, director of The Center for Bioethics and Human Dignity. At least in theory, that is.

"If you asked about personhood," Kilner says, "people will say, in theory, they support full personhood at conception— few people would deny that." In practice, though, Kilner says many Christians also would "make some exceptions for abortion in the case of genetic deficiencies, or for the use of stem cells. And this is from people whom you'd expect to hold pro-life positions."

To make that distinction, he says, is to bestow personhood at a later stage in development.

One complicating factor for conferring personhood at conception is that a large number of fertilized eggs do not implant, says Hessel Bouma III, professor of biology at Calvin College and chairman of the bioethics commission of the American Scientific Affiliation [a Christian organization of scientists]. Estimates of the number of fertilized eggs that fail to implant run as high as 70 percent.

Conservative Christians have been reluctant to face this fact, Bouma says.

"It's something we've only become aware of in the last 30 years—the majority of fertilized eggs fail to develop," he says. "If we consider the fertilized egg as a person, then take all of the other causes of death and multiply them by three—that's the number of so-called persons who are dying before developing."

Bouma says that personhood should be conferred during the second trimester of pregnancy. Before that point, he says, too many things can go wrong. But most evangelicals, such as Robert D. Orr, director of ethics at the University of Vermont College of Medicine, tie personhood closer to conception.

Focus on Conception

At one time Orr considered personhood to begin at implantation of the fertilized egg in the uterus. But threats posed by advances in biotechnology have made him reconsider.

"I think it's important to hold the line for moral standing to start at conception," Orr says. "If you move the line away from conception, it just opens up the door to so many technological advances."

Orr first became involved in bioethics following the *Roe v. Wade* decision in the 1970s [which legalized abortion]. He eventually gave up his medical practice in Vermont, where he'd practiced for 20 years, and enrolled in the University of Chicago to study bioethics.

He has studied personhood as it relates to both the beginning and end of life. Vermont has been targeted by the Hemlock Society as the second state (after Oregon) where a "death with dignity" bill, which he opposes, could be introduced.

Orr and his colleague, C. Christopher Hook of the Mayo Clinic, have written an essay in the *Yale Journal of Health Policy, Law, and Ethics* entitled "Stem-Cell Research: Magical Promise vs. Moral Peril." They argue for recognizing a unique human individual at the earliest stages of life.

In the abortion debate, they write, it is ironic that "many argue that it is not a human until it is 'out of the uterus,' and in the stem-cell debate many argue that it is not a human until it is 'in the uterus.' These arguments based on the individual's location are feeble attempts to deny the basic fact understood and accepted by scientists for many generations: humanhood begins with the union of 23 chromosomes from the ovum with 23 chromosomes from the sperm."

Most Christian ethicists that *Christianity Today* interviewed hold that personhood begins at conception. Like Kilner, though, many of them note that the practices of evangelicals don't always reflect that view.

For example, during the in vitro fertilization (IVF) process, embryos are frozen, rated for their quality, discarded if they hold genetic defects, or thawed and dumped in the trash if they are no longer needed. None of these practices would be acceptable in the case of fully developed persons. But most are accepted by evangelicals undergoing IVF treatments.

The scale of IVF and other assisted reproductive technologies (ART) is also a concern. In 2001, the last year for which statistics are available, the Centers for Disease Control reported there were 107,587 ART attempts (known as cycles) resulting in 40,687 babies. That total is up from 64,724 cycles and 20,659 babies in 1996.

With an average cost of $12,400 per cycle, infertility treatment has become a billion-dollar industry. And there's enormous potential for growth. The Association for Reproductive Medicine reports that only 5 percent of the estimated 2.1 million infertile couples have used IVF. To capitalize on this potential, a number of clinics have begun offering "100 percent money-back guarantees" and financing for patients who sign up for ART discount packages.

Concerned about the cost of IVF, the alarming number of excess embryos in fertility clinic freezers, and a tendency to view children as commodities, ethicists have begun calling for limits on ART. A United Methodist bioethics panel recommended to that church's General Assembly in early May [2004] that couples forgo the use of IVF—or at least severely limit the number of embryos produced.

Against Fertility Treatments

A member of the committee, Amy Laura Hall, adamantly opposes IVF. An ordained Methodist minister and assistant professor of theological ethics at Duke Divinity School, Hall anguishes in her opposition. She has several friends who resorted to IVF; she adores their children.

She tells of a close friend who was "very much pro-life" before facing infertility. As a result of her IVF treatment, the friend began to rethink her positions on the beginning of life.

"It became really clear, as we were looking at the embryo under the microscope, that life must not begin at conception," she told Hall after completing her IVF process.

Hall believes that the rationalistic and impersonal practices of IVF—watching the sperm and egg join under a microscope, rating and discarding lower-quality embryos, and freezing those left over—undermine respect for life and the concept that life begins at conception.

"We think that abortion is something that bad women do . . . or something that irresponsible teenagers do. On the other hand, IVF is something that good, respectable Christian couples do to grow their families," she says. "They are willing to go to great expense, to scrimp and to save, for the procedures that will give them children. Is it possible that what's going on with IVF is very subtly evil?"

IVF undermines the value of human life and paves the way for using embryos as raw material for biotechnology, Hall argues. In coming years, she believes, evangelicals will face a test of resolve on the question of prenatal life.

"For years, evangelical leaders have been very clear on the question of life and personhood beginning at conception," Hall says. "Now that we have found a use for embryos, with the possibility of healing ourselves and healing our children, we are tempted to rethink our position on prenatal life." She points to an irony of the evangelical pro-life commitment: "Now that we are being called to bear the sacrifice of a witness to life, we are tempted not to sacrifice."

Despite the concerns of Hall and other members of the United Methodist bioethics committee, their recommendations about forgoing IVF—and any reference to the embryo as "a form of human life"—were eliminated from the bioethics resolution passed at the latest General Conference.

The Conference passed an additional committee recommendation that excess embryos be used for stem-cell research. Hall co-wrote a dissent from that position.

"We must repent for our actions in creating these embryos," she says, "and then allow them to thaw with a sense of grief and loss. To make use of them allows us to avoid the realization that something indeed has been lost."

A Different Approach

Hook, who teaches ethics at the Mayo Clinic, is also concerned about the practices of IVF. But he believes those practices should be reformed, rather than halted.

One alternative is to limit the number of fertilized eggs to only the number that a couple will implant.

Stunningly, technology also can be harnessed for a lesser-known alternative. Clinics can freeze fertilized eggs at the pronuclear stage—before the sperm and egg DNA are fused.

"If we cryo-preserve at that point," Hook says, "we don't have as much worry about the loss of life."

This technique further muddies the issue of when human life and personhood begin. In any case, Hook says, such reforms mean Christian couples have to be specific about their beliefs when talking with doctors.

The medical community's concept of personhood varies sharply from the most prevalent Christian views. Bob Scheidt, chair of the Christian Medical Association ethics commission, says the medical profession uses four characteristics to define personhood.

All four are related to the function of the neocortex of the brain: rationality, self-awareness, communication/relationship with others, and happiness. Scheidt believes that these functions fall short of a true definition of personhood.

Some of them, like self-awareness and rationality, disappear when a person is under anesthesia, for example. Does that make a patient under anesthesia any less of a person?

Like many ethicists, Scheidt is concerned that personhood is used more often than not to exclude, rather than include people.

Image of God

"When we didn't want to treat blacks as equal," he says, "we defined them as not persons or as three-fifths of a person in the early American Constitution. We define a fetus as a non-person, and then we can do whatever we wish with it. Most recently [personhood has] been used in arguments about people in persistent vegetative states."

Scheidt believes that the issue of ensoulment is less important than that of the image of God.

"We are bearers of an alien dignity," he says. "We bear the image of God—we are more than phenomena of the earth."

Gilbert Meilaender, professor of Christian ethics at Valparaiso University, says we must restore the notion that a person is something more than a set of capacities.

Instead, he argues that all human life has value because God cares for it regardless of capacities.

For example, he says, while a Scriptural passage like Psalm 139:13–16 ("You knit me together in my mother's womb . . .") may not be a "proof text" for personhood at conception, it does show that "God's care and his hand are on those who have no capacities."

Because we are of equal dignity, according to Meilaender, we are not at each other's disposal.

Any attempt to separate personhood from human being undermines this essential human dignity. Ironically, he says, U.S. society has limited the idea of personhood in order to narrow its moral responsibility. "The class of human beings," he notes, "has come to be much larger than the class of persons."

Christian theology can offer a corrective to that limited view of personhood, Meilaender believes. By articulating the value of all human beings, he says, "We will be able to show the way in which the language of personhood is confused and dangerous."

Allen Verhey, who chairs the department of religion at Hope College in Holland, Michigan, offers a theological perspective that agrees on the dangers of mere humanistic criteria for personhood.

Verhey sees a parallel between the parable of the Good Samaritan and the debate over personhood. The questions "Who is a person?" and "Who is a neighbor?" both have the same goal—"to find out where our moral duties end," he says.

"Jesus doesn't give a set of criteria to define who is a neighbor," Verhey says. "In the same way, I don't think we can give a set of criteria to define who a person is."

Pro-Life Biology

At the President's Council on Bioethics, William Hurlbut of Stanford University approaches the issue of individual status from a biological perspective.

He never discusses the soul, and only rarely does he bring up personhood.

Instead, he asks: "When does the embryo become one of us? When does it become an individual with moral standing?"

Hurlbut, who focuses on the ethics of biotechnology, argues that biology can show when an embryo is worthy of full moral status.

"It's undeniable that you have biological continuity in the unfolding of a life," he says. "Fertilization initiates the most complex chemical reaction in the known universe—once initiated, you have a transformation from a zygote (fertilized egg) to an organism with an integrated, self-directed, self-assembling trajectory of a life."

Ethicists often refer to the human embryo as a "potential human being." Hurlbut balks at this characterization, objecting to potential being confused with mere possibility. Rather, he says a human embryo has "potential as potency."

"It's a living entity," he says. "The embryo is a self-assembling individual that is on organizational continuity with the later fetal stage, the baby at the breast, the teenager—all the way to natural death, you have a continuous, unbroken continuity of being."

The real drive behind the argument over personhood, at least for human embryos, says Hurlbut, is that they have become a potential resource for biotechnology.

"If there was no use for the embryo," he argues, "people would be more willing to grant it full moral standing from the beginning."

Beyond conception, the next scientific threshold for moral standing comes at 14 days. That's when the primitive streak, a precursor of the spinal column, appears in an embryo. Before then, Hurlbut says, embryos have been seen as "inchoate compost cells" or simply raw material for the developing life.

But new research into mammalian embryology, he says, shows "there is already development in the individual embryo at its earliest stages."

Moral Status of Twins

Fourteen days is also when "twinning" can no longer occur; that is, until that point the embryo could split and become identical twins. Consequently, many argue that until this point the embryo is not an individual person. But Hurlbut says the potential for twinning has no bearing on the embryo's humanity.

"The moral standing doesn't change with twinning," he says. "You had one human life, and now you've got two human lives." Twinning occurs when the embryo "is disrupted and heals itself," he says. (This process happens 10 times more often in IVF labs than in ordinary development in the womb, he says.)

This purely biological view is a kind of twin to the theological view espoused by evangelicals such as Susan Haack, a Wisconsin OB-GYN and member of the ethics commission of the Christian Medical Association. She says that, biblically, she cannot separate human life from personhood.

Based on one part each of theology, ethics, and biology, she traces personhood back to those first stages of life. After conception, she says, "you have the same being all the way to birth and beyond."

Her theology echoes Roman Catholic teaching.

"From the moment of conception," the 1987 encyclical *Donum Vitae* says, "the life of every human being is to be respected in an absolute way because man is the only creature on earth that God has wished for himself and the spiritual soul of each man is 'immediately created' by God; his whole being bears the image of the Creator."

Susan Barg learned this truth firsthand from her son Aaron. After he was born, her gynecologist told her that he would have counseled her to have an abortion had he known beforehand about Aaron's Trisomy 13.

Barg says she would have found a way to follow her doctor's advice and justify ending Aaron's life. Now she can't imagine making that decision.

"Having Aaron here has helped me understand that God doesn't make mistakes," Susan says. "Aaron has a mission on this earth to fulfill, and a purpose—just like you and I have."

Reproductive Technologies Are Moral

Brian Doyle

The Roman Catholic Church has taken a firm stance against in vitro fertilization (IVF). This has caused dissension among some Catholics, particularly in the United States. In the following selection Brian Doyle, one of those dissenting Catholics explains why he feels the church's position is wrong. Doyle begins by describing his baby daughter, Lily, the product of IVF. He acknowledges that according to the church, Lily was conceived through immoral means. The main reason for the church's objection, Doyle says, is that IVF separates conception from a loving sexual union. However, he argues, he and his wife did lovingly bring Lily into the world. He relates the experience he and his wife went through. Like many infertile women, she had blocked fallopian tubes. Despite corrective surgery, her tubes remained blocked. The couple considered adoption but followed their desire to have a child of their own by trying IVF. Despite all the theological condemnations of the procedure, Doyle says, their daughter is a miracle, conceived out of love. Thus, he concludes, IVF is morally justified. Essayist and author Brian Doyle has been a frequent contributor to U.S. Catholic.

I am lying on the floor watching my daughter, Lily, pick up a rattle. She is 3 months old and has never done this before. She regards the prey carefully for some minutes before suddenly sending her hands out on their expedition. The left hand arrives first; the right hand gets sidetracked and ends up caressing the carpet. After a brief period of uncertainty, her hand grips the rattle, and Lily hoists it into the air like a miniature barbell. She grins, a huge and toothless grin, and begins to chirp like a sparrow. I applaud; even the smallest miracles deserve recognition.

A baby, a rattle, and a fawning father are nothing new. All new parents are intrinsically prone to musing about the miraculous, since new life is the most miraculous item on the menu. And although Lily's Herculean efforts to harness her motor skills are astonishing to me, they are only the opening notes of what will, I hope, be a continuous symphony of graceful acts. Why, then, do I feel that this first autonomous act is such an extraordinary little miracle? I feel this enormously. As I lie there on the floor, smiling, and clapping gently, I can feel myself close to tears.

I think it is because I consider Lily herself to be a miracle of unusual proportions. She is a child conceived by *in vitro* fertilization (IVF), a "test-tube baby," in the harsh colloquial phrase of the day. She was not conceived in the warm womb of my tiny wife. She was conceived in a small glass dish in a suburban medical clinic a day after several eggs were taken from my wife's ovaries and several million sperm cells were contributed by me. From the dish she traveled by pipette back into my wife from whom she emerged mewling three months ago.

An Unnatural Child

By the standards of the Roman Catholic Church, Lily is an unnatural child conceived by a "morally illicit" technique that separates procreation from the union of husband and wife. "The church remains opposed from the moral point of view to *in vitro* fertilization," concludes the "Instruction on Respect for Human Life in Its Origin and on the Dignity of Procreation," a publication issued by the Congregation for the Doctrine of the Faith in 1987.

The official opposition of the church to IVF rests on the guiding principle behind *Humanae vitae*, Pope Paul VI's 1968 encyclical; namely, that sex, love, and procreation are inseparable. Sexual intercourse is an expression of marital love, wrote Paul, and each sexual act must be generally open to the possibility of procreation. Because IVF divorces procreation from sexual union, it's wrong. In other words, a child conceived by means other than a loving sexual act is conceived illicitly from a moral standpoint.

There are other objections to the procedure. One is that the dignity of the new human life is violated by the intervention of the medical professionals who oversee fertilization and implant the embryo in the woman. Another is that the process sometimes entails the creation of several embryos, which are (depending on the IVF clinic) implanted all at once or frozen for later IVF efforts. To freeze an embryo is to treat life with disrespect, say church spokespersons; to allow several embryos to die *in utero* is what *New World* columnist Father John Dietzen calls "a deliberate destruction of human life."

But it is on the inseparability of sex and procreation that the church rests its formal objection to IVF, says Father Richard McCormick, S.J. of the University of Notre Dame. "The church disapproves of IVF on the same grounds that it disapproves of contraception: that is, that love, sex, and procreation are inseparable. Because IVF separates sex and procreation, it's considered illicit, no matter what the circumstances may be."

No Other Way to Conceive

Let me tell you about the circumstances. My wife and I were married five years ago. Our marriage is rich and funny and poignant. We awaited children with trepidation and excitement, awed and thrilled at the chance to bathe a new soul in our coupled love. Month after month we hoped. Month after month we were disappointed. We went to a doctor to see whether there was a medical reason for our childlessness. There was; my wife's fallopian tubes were blocked by scar tissue. She had an operation to undo the damage; it only confirmed the permanence of the blockage.

I remember sitting in the doctor's office and hearing her say that we would not be able to have children of our own. I remember that her voice was gentle, but that her words cut like razors. I remember that my wife's face grew sad and gray.

We registered with several adoption agencies; we got second and third and fourth opinions; my wife readied herself for more complicated surgical procedures; and we began to seriously consider *in vitro* fertilization. We thought about selfishness; at what point, we thought, are we pursuing parenthood too assiduously? When is it that you decide to stop trying to be the parents of your own child? We also thought about cost, about morality, and about the procedure's relatively low success rate (about 10 percent of women who undergo implantation of fertilized eggs give birth). And then we went ahead with the procedure.

A year later there is Lily.

"[IVF] is a subversion of the dignity and unity of marriage," says Dietzen in his column in the *New World*.

"[IVF] deprives human procreation of the dignity which is proper and connatural to it," say the authors of the "Instruction on Respect for Human Life in Its Origin and on the Dignity of Procreation."

"The child is not the fruit of intimacy, but the product of a scientific procedure," says Father John Connery, S.J. of Loyola University in Chicago, Illinois.

Lily makes another stab at the rattle again with her left hand. This time, however, she brings it slowly and carefully to her mouth. She spends the next few minutes happily trying to eat it.

Dignity, zygotes, subversion, illicit, procreation. Words, words, words. The reality is Lily, and she is holy beyond my comprehension and yours and Father Dietzen's and the authors of the "Instruction on Respect for Human Life in Its Origin and on the Dignity of Procreation," and the pope's. She is a miracle, pure and simple; and how she came about doesn't make a whole lot of difference to me. If holiness is in life— and that is the pervading principle of Christianity, the principle by which abortion is banned, the principle by which birth control is proscribed—then this life is holy, and to forbid the means by which it came about is, I think foolish and cruel. Do we ban scientific intervention in other medical areas? Are heart transplants immoral? Are cesarean sections?

Unrealistic Ruling

My anger at foolishness doesn't prevent me from understanding what well-meaning authors are trying to say when they staunchly defend the church's stance on IVF. We must adhere to principles, they say; otherwise, we're adrift in areas of incredible moral confusion. What about surrogate motherhood? What about donated sperm? What about genetic engineering? Where do we draw the line?

I don't know. But I sometimes think the church is very good at drawing lines. It seems to me that this particular line, the one drawn between married couples and their children, is a remarkably stupid one. It joins procreation and the conjugal act so tightly that it leaves no room for reality. My wife and I could not have children in the same way most parents have children. But now we have a child, a daughter so gentle and beautiful she breaks my heart every day. Did we do something wrong? The church tells me that the procedure by which Lily came to be is morally illicit. I disagree; I think it is a miracle, and I think the church hierarchy is lost in a dusty corner of the Moral Mansion, far away from where people live and far away from the things people carry in their hearts.

Having thoroughly gummed her rattle, Lily is now absorbed in the clowns tattooed on her blanket. She waves her fingers over them like a tiny magician. I chirp, just for fun, and Lily looks up at me. We stare at each other for a moment. On her face an enormous smile appears. She laughs, a sound like the crisp note of an alto saxophone, and my heart breaks again into thousands of pieces.

I laugh, too, and then I begin to clap gently. I do so because I think miracles should be applauded, not forbidden.

Human Reproductive Cloning Is Unethical

President's Council on Bioethics

No reliable report of a cloned human baby has yet been published, but the possibility of human cloning has generated enormous controversy. In the following selection a presidential advisory panel on medical and biological ethics presents its reasons for opposing cloning to produce children. The President's Council on Bioethics denies that people have a right to have a child by any means possible. One major objection to the idea of cloning humans is that it may be risky for the baby. Cloned animals often experience serious health problems, including premature aging. Another objection involves consent. Since a person cannot give consent to a medical procedure before being born, such a procedure would be unethical. The council also expresses concern that women will be exploited for their eggs should human cloning become a reality. President George W. Bush created the council on November 28, 2001, to advise him on bioethical issues that emerge as a consequence of advances in biomedical science and technology. It is headed by physician and bioethicist Leon Kass, who is affiliated with the University of Chicago and the American Enterprise Institute.

The prospect of cloning-to-produce-children raises a host of moral questions, among them the following: Could the first attempts to clone a human child be made without violating accepted moral norms governing experimentation on human subjects? What harms might be inflicted on the cloned child as a consequence of having been made a clone? Is it significant that the cloned child would inherit a genetic identity lived in advance by another—and, in some cases, the genetic identity of the cloned child's rearing parent? Is it significant

President's Council on Bioethics, *Human Cloning and Human Dignity: An Ethical Inquiry*, www.bioethics.gov, July 2002.

that cloned children would be the first human beings whose genetic identity was entirely known and selected in advance? How might cloning-to-produce-children affect relationships within the cloning families? More generally, how might it affect the relationship between the generations? How might it affect the way society comes to view children? What other prospects would we be tacitly approving in advance by accepting this practice? What important human goods might be enhanced or sacrificed were we to approve cloning-to-produce-children?

In what follows, we shall explicitly consider many of these questions. But as we do so, we shall not lose sight of the larger and fundamental human contexts. . . . Indeed, overarching our entire discussion of the *specific* ethical issues is our concern for the human significance of procreation as a whole and our desire to protect what is valuable in it from erosion and degradation—not just from cloning but from other possible technological and nontechnological dangers. . . .

Unpersuaded by Arguments

While we as a Council acknowledge merit in some of the arguments made for cloning-to-produce-children, we are generally not persuaded by them. The fundamental weakness of the proponents' case is found in their incomplete view of human procreation and families, and especially the place and well-being of children. Proponents of cloning tend to see procreation primarily as the free exercise of a parental right, namely, a right to satisfy parental desires for self-fulfillment or a right to have a child who is healthy or "superior." Parents seek to overcome obstacles to reproduction, to keep their children free of genetic disease or disorder, and to provide them with the best possible genetic endowment. The principles guiding such prospective parents are freedom (for themselves), control (over their child), and well-being (both for themselves and what they imagine is best for their child). Even taken together, these principles provide at best only a partial understanding of the meaning and entailments of human procreation and child-rearing. In practice, they may prove to undermine the very goods that the proponents of cloning aim to serve, by undermining the unconditional acceptance of one's offspring that is so central to parenthood.

There are a number of objections—or at the very least limitations—to viewing cloning-to-produce-children through the prism of rights. Basic human rights are usually asserted on behalf of the human individual agent: for example, a meaningful right not to be prevented from bearing a child can be asserted for each individual against state-mandated sterilization programs. But the act of procreation is not an act involving a single individual. Indeed, until human cloning arrives, it continues to be impossible for any one person to procreate alone. More important, there is a crucial third party involved: the child, whose centrality to the activity exposes the insufficiency of thinking about procreation in terms of rights.

After all, rights are limited in the following crucial way: they cannot be ethically exercised at the expense of the rights of another. But the "right to reproduce" cannot be ethically exercised without at least considering the child that such exercise will bring into being and who is at risk of harm and injustice from the exercise. This obligation cannot be waived by an appeal to the absolutist argument of the goodness of existence. Yes, existence is a primary good, but that does not diminish the ethical significance of knowingly and willfully putting a child in grave physical danger in the very act of giving that child existence. It is certainly true that a life with even severe disability may well be judged worth living by its bearer: "It is better to have been born as I am than not to be here at all." But if his or her disability was caused by behavior that could have been avoided by parents (for example, by not drinking or using drugs during pregnancy, or, arguably, by not cloning), many would argue that they should have avoided it.

A post-facto affirmation of existence by the harmed child would not retroactively excuse the parental misconduct that caused the child's disability, nor would it justify their failure to think of the child's well-being as they went about exercising their "right to procreate." Indeed, procreation is, by its very nature, a limitation of absolute rights, since it brings into existence another human being toward whom we have responsibilities and duties.

In short, the right to decide *"whether* to bear or beget a child" does not include a right to have a child *by whatever means.* Nor can this right be said to imply a corollary—the right to decide what kind of child one is going to have. There are at least some circumstances where reproductive freedom must be limited to protect the good of the child (as, for instance, with the ban on incest). Our society's commitment to freedom and parental authority by no means implies that all innovative procedures and practices should be allowed or accepted, no matter how bizarre or dangerous.

Unforeseen Consequences

Proponents of cloning, when they do take into account the interests of the child, sometimes argue that this interest justifies and even requires thoroughgoing parental control over the procreative process. Yet this approach, even when well intentioned, may undermine the good of the child more than it serves the child's best interests. For one thing, cloning-to-produce-children of a desired or worthy sort overlooks the need to restrain the parental temptation to total mastery over children. It is especially morally dubious for this project to go forward when we know so little about the unforeseen and unintended consequences of exercising such genetic control. In trying by cloning to circumvent the risk of genetic disease or to promote particular traits, it is possible—perhaps likely—that new risks to the cloned child's health and fitness would be inadvertently introduced (including the forgoing of genetic novelty, a known asset in the constant struggle against microbial and parasitic diseases). Parental control is a double-edged sword, and proponents seem not to acknowledge the harms, both physical and psychological, that may befall the child whose genetic identity is selected in advance.

The case for cloning in the name of the child's health and well-being is certainly the strongest and most compelling. The desire that one's child be free from a given genetic disease is a worthy aspiration. We recognize there may be some unusual or extreme cases in which cloning might be the best means to serve this moral good, if other ethical obstacles could somehow be overcome. (A few of us also believe that the desire to give a child "improved" or "superior" genetic equipment is not necessarily to be condemned.) However, such aspirations could endanger the personal, familial, and societal goods supported by the character of human procreation. We are willing to grant that there may be exceptional cases in which cloning-to-produce-children is morally defensible; however, that being said, we would also argue that such cases do not justify the harmful experiments and social problems that might be entailed by engaging in human cloning. Hard cases are said to make bad law. The same would be true for succumbing to the rare, sentimentally appealing case in which cloning seems morally plausible.

Finally, proponents do not adequately face up to the difficulty of how "well-being" is to be defined. Generally, they argue that these matters are to be left up to the free choices of parents and doctors. But this means that the judgments of "proper" and "improper" will be made according to subjective criteria alone, and under such circumstances, it will be almost impossible to rule out certain "improvements" as unacceptable.

The Case Against Cloning

In the sections that follow, we shall explain more fully why

Members of the Council are not convinced by the arguments for cloning-to-produce-children, even in the most defensible cases. To see why this is so, we need to consider cloning-to-produce-children from the broadest possible moral perspective, beginning with ethical questions regarding experiments on human subjects. What we hope to show is that the frequently made safety arguments strike deeper than we usually realize, and that they point beyond themselves toward more fundamental moral objections to cloning-to-produce-children.

We begin with concerns regarding the safety of the cloning procedure and the health of the participants. We do so for several reasons. First, these concerns are widely, indeed nearly unanimously, shared. Second, they lend themselves readily to familiar modes of ethical analysis—including concerns about harming the innocent, protecting human rights, and ensuring the consent of all research subjects. Finally, if carefully considered, these concerns begin to reveal the important ethical principles that must guide our broader assessment of cloning-to-produce-children. They suggest that human beings, unlike inanimate matter or even animals, are in some way *inviolable,* and therefore challenge us to reflect on what it is *about* human beings that makes them inviolable, and whether cloning-to-produce-children threatens these distinctly human goods.

In initiating this analysis, there is perhaps no better place to start than the long-standing international practice of regulating experiments on human subjects. After all, the cloning of a human being, as well as all the research and trials required before such a procedure could be expected to succeed, would constitute experiments on the individuals involved—the egg donor, the birthing mother, and especially the child-to-be. It therefore makes sense to consider the safety and health concerns that arise from cloning-to-produce-children in light of the widely shared ethical principles that govern experimentation on human subjects. . . .

Ethical Codes

The ethics of research on human subjects suggest three sorts of problems that would arise in cloning-to-produce-children: (1) problems of safety; (2) a special problem of consent; and (3) problems of exploitation of women and the just distribution of risk. We shall consider each in turn.

Problems of Safety

First, cloning-to-produce-children is not now safe. Concerns about the safety of the individuals involved in a cloning procedure are shared by nearly everyone on all sides of the cloning debate. Even most proponents of cloning-to-produce-children generally qualify their support with a caveat about the safety of the procedure. Cloning experiments in other mammals strongly suggest that cloning-to-produce-children is, at least for now, far too risky to attempt. Safety concerns revolve around potential dangers to the cloned child, as well as to the egg donor and the woman who would carry the cloned child to birth.

(a) Risks to the child. Risks to the cloned child-to-be must be taken especially seriously, both because they are most numerous and most serious and because—unlike the risks to the egg donor and birth mother—they cannot be accepted knowingly and freely by the person who will bear them. In animal experiments to date, only a small percentage of implanted clones have resulted in live births, and a substantial portion of those live-born clones have suffered complications that proved fatal fairly quickly. Some serious though nonfatal abnormalities in cloned animals have also been observed, including substantially increased birth-size, liver and brain defects, and lung, kidney, and cardiovascular problems.

Longer-term consequences are of course not known, as the oldest successfully cloned mammal is only six years of age. Medium-term consequences, including premature aging immune system failure, and sudden unexplained death, have already become apparent in some cloned mammals. Some researchers have also expressed concerns that a donor nucleus from an individual who has lived for some years may have accumulated genetic mutations that—if the nucleus were used in the cloning of a new human life—may predispose the new individual to certain sorts of cancer and other diseases.

(b) Risks to the egg donor and the birth mother. Accompanying the threats to the cloned child's health and well-being are risks to the health of the egg donors. These include risks to her future reproductive health caused by the hormonal treatments required for egg retrieval and general health risks resulting from the necessary superovulation.

Animal studies also suggest the likelihood of health risks to the woman who carries the cloned fetus to term. The animal data suggest that late-term fetal losses and spontaneous abortions occur substantially more often with cloned fetuses than in natural pregnancies. In humans, such late-term fetal losses may lead to substantially increased maternal morbidity and mortality. In addition, animal studies have shown that many pregnancies involving cloned fetuses result in serious complications, including toxemia and excessive fluid accumulation in the uterus, both of which pose risks to the pregnant animal's health. In one prominent cattle cloning study, just under one-third of the pregnant cows died from complications late in pregnancy.

Reflecting on the dangers to birth mothers in animal cloning studies, the National Academy report concluded:

> Results of animal studies suggest that reproductive cloning of humans would similarly pose a high risk to the health of both fetus or infant and mother and lead to associated psychological risks for the mother as a consequence of late spontaneous abortions or the birth of a stillborn child or a child with severe health problems.

(c) An abiding moral concern. Because of these risks, there is widespread agreement that, at least for now, attempts at

cloning-to-produce-children would constitute unethical experimentation on human subjects and are therefore impermissible. These safety considerations were alone enough to lead the National Bioethics Advisory Commission in June 1997 to call for a temporary prohibition of human cloning-to-produce-children. Similar concerns, based on almost five more years of animal experimentation, convinced the panel of the National Academy of Sciences in January 2002 that the United States should ban such cloning for at least five years.

Efforts at Safety Are Dubious

Past discussions of this subject have often given the impression that the safety concern is a purely temporary one that can be allayed in the near future, as scientific advances and improvements in technique reduce the risks to an ethically acceptable level. But this impression is mistaken, for considerable safety risks are likely to be enduring, perhaps permanent. If so, there will be abiding ethical difficulties *even with efforts aimed at making human cloning safe.*

The reason is clear: experiments to develop new reproductive technologies are necessarily intergenerational, undertaken to serve the reproductive desires of prospective parents but practiced also and always upon prospective children. Any such experiment unavoidably involves risks to the child-to-be, a being who is both the *product* and also the most vulnerable human *subject* of the research. Exposed to risk during the extremely sensitive life-shaping processes of his or her embryological development, any child-to-be is a singularly vulnerable creature, one maximally deserving of protection against risk of experimental (and other) harm. If experiments to learn how to clone a child are ever to be ethical, the degree of risk to that child-to-be would have to be extremely low, arguably no greater than for children-to-be who are conceived from union of egg and sperm. It is extremely unlikely that this moral burden can be met, not for decades if at all.

In multiple experiments involving six of the mammalian species cloned to date, more than 89 percent of the cloned embryos transferred to recipient females did not come to birth, and many of the live-born cloned animals are or become abnormal. If success means achieving normal and healthy development not just at birth but throughout the life span, there is even less reason for confidence. The oldest cloned mammal (Dolly) is only six years old[1] and has exhibited unusually early arthritis. The reasons for failure in animal cloning are not well understood. Also, no nonhuman primates have been cloned. It will be decades (at least) before we could obtain positive evidence that cloned primates might live a normal healthy (primate) life.

Even a high success rate in animals would not suffice by itself to make human trials morally acceptable. In addition to the usual uncertainties in jumping the gap from animal to human research, cloning is likely to present particularly difficult problems of interspecies difference. Animal experiments have already shown substantial differences in the reproductive success of identical cloning techniques used in different species. If these results represent species-specific differences in, for example, the ease of epigenetic reprogramming and imprinting of the donor DNA, the magnitude of the risks to the child-to-be of the first human cloning experiments would be unknown and potentially large, no matter how much success had been achieved in animals. There can in principle be no direct experimental evidence sufficient for assessing the degree of such risk.

Can a highly reduced risk of deformity, disease, and premature death in animal cloning, coupled with the inherently unpredictable risk of moving from animals to humans, ever be low enough to meet the ethically acceptable standard set by reproduction begun with egg and sperm? The answer, as a

1. Dolly has since died.

matter of necessity, can never be better than "Just possibly." Given the severity of the possible harms involved in human cloning, and given that those harms fall on the very vulnerable child-to-be, such an answer would seem to be enduringly inadequate.

Comparison with IVF

Similar arguments, it is worth noting, were made before the first attempts at human in vitro fertilization. People suggested that it would be unethical experimentation even to try to determine whether IVF could be safely done. And then, of course, IVF was accomplished. Eventually, it became a common procedure, and today the moral argument about its safety seems to many people beside the point. Yet the fact of success in that case does not establish precedent in this one, nor does it mean that the first attempts at IVF were not in fact unethical experiments upon the unborn, despite the fortunate results.

Be this as it may, the case of cloning is genuinely different. With IVF, assisted fertilization of egg by sperm immediately releases a developmental process, linked to the sexual union of the two gametes, that nature has selected over millions of years for the entire mammalian line. But in cloning experiments to produce children, researchers would be transforming a sexual system into an asexual one, a change that requires major and "unnatural" reprogramming of donor DNA if there is to be any chance of success. They are neither enabling nor restoring a natural process, and the alterations involved are such that success in one species cannot be presumed to predict success in another. Moreover, any new somatic mutations in the donor cell's chromosomal DNA would be passed along to the cloned child-to-be and its offspring. Here we can see even more the truly intergenerational character of cloning experimentation, and this should justify placing the highest moral burden of persuasion on those who would like to proceed with efforts to make cloning safe for producing children. (By reminding us of the need to protect the lives and well-being of our children and our children's children, this broader analysis of the safety question points toward larger moral objections to producing cloned children. . . .)

It therefore appears to us that, given the dangers involved and the relatively limited goods to be gained from cloning-to-produce-children, conducting experiments in an effort to make cloning-to-produce-children safer would itself be an unacceptable violation of the norms of the ethics of research. *There seems to be no ethical way to try to discover whether cloning-to-produce-children can become safe, now or in the future.*

A Special Problem of Consent

A further concern relating to the ethics of human research revolves around the question of consent. Consent from the cloned child-to-be is of course impossible to obtain, and because no one consents to his or her own birth, it may be argued that concerns about consent are misplaced when applied to the unborn. But the issue is not so simple. For reasons having to do both with the safety concerns raised above and with social, psychological, and moral concerns . . . , an attempt to clone a human being would potentially expose a cloned individual-to-be to great risks of harm, quite distinct from those accompanying other sorts of reproduction. Given the risks, and the fact that consent cannot be obtained, the ethically correct choice may be to avoid the experiment. The fact that those engaged in cloning cannot ask an unconceived child for permission places a burden on the cloners, not on the child. Given that anyone considering creating a cloned child must know that he or she is putting a newly created human life at exceptional risk, the burden on the would-be cloners seems clear: they must make a compelling case why the procedure should not be avoided altogether.

Reflections on the purpose and meaning of seeking consent support this point. Why, after all, does society insist upon consent as an essential principle of the ethics of scientific research? Along with honoring the free will of the subject, we insist on consent to protect the weak and the vulnerable, and in particular to protect them from the powerful. It would therefore be morally questionable, at the very least, to choose to impose potentially grave harm on an individual especially in the very act of giving that individual life. Giving existence to a human being does not grant one the right to maim or harm that human being in research.

Problems of Exploitation of Women

Cloning-to-produce-children may also lead to the exploitation of women who would be called upon to donate oocytes. Widespread use of the techniques of cloning-to-produce-children would require large numbers of eggs. Animal models suggest that several hundred eggs may be required before one attempt at cloning can be successful. The required oocytes would have to be donated, and the process of making them available would involve hormonal treatments to induce superovulation. If financial incentives are offered, they might lead poor women especially to place themselves at risk in this way (and might also compromise the voluntariness of their "choice" to make donations). Thus, research on cloning-to-produce-children could impose disproportionate burdens on women, particularly low-income women.

These questions of the ethics of research—particularly the issue of physical safety—point clearly to the conclusion that cloning-to-produce-children is unacceptable. In reaching this conclusion, we join the National Bioethics Advisory Commission and the National Academy of Sciences. But we go beyond the findings of those distinguished bodies in also pointing to the dangers that will *always* be inherent in the very process of trying to make cloning-to-produce-children safer. On this ground, we conclude that the problem of safety is not a temporary ethical concern. It is rather an enduring moral concern that might not be surmountable and should thus preclude work toward the development of cloning techniques to produce children. In light of the risks and other ethical concerns raised by this form of human experimentation, *we therefore conclude that cloning-to-produce-children should not be attempted.*

Human Reproductive Cloning Is Ethical

Raanan Gillon

The prospect of human reproductive cloning has led to the passage of numerous legal bans on the hypothetical procedure. In the following selection, medical professor Raanan Gillon rebuts the principal arguments for a permanent ban on human reproductive cloning. He acknowledges that many people have a gut reaction against cloning but says that gut feelings cannot be trusted as the basis of sound policy anymore than revulsion at the cutting open of another person can be considered an argument against surgery. Furthermore, according to Gillon, some critics say that it is wrong to produce children with the same genetic identity as someone else, but this argument fails to acknowledge the acceptance of identical twins, who have the same genes. Gillon asserts that choosing to have a baby through cloning does not necessarily mean robbing that baby of respect or dignity. A cloned child could be treated as respectfully as any other child, given the will to do so. Raanan Gillon is a professor in the Medical Ethics Unit of the University of London School of Medicine.

Human reproductive cloning—replication of genetically identical or near identical human beings—can hardly be said to have had a good press. Banned in one way or another by many countries including the United Kingdom, execrated by the General Assembly of the World Health Organization as "ethically unacceptable and contrary to human integrity and morality," forbidden by the European Commission through its Biotechnology Patents Directive, by the Council of Europe through its Bioethics Convention, and by UNESCO through

Raanan Gillon, "Human Reproductive Cloning: A Look at the Arguments Against It and a Rejection of Most of Them," *The Journal of the Royal Society of Medicine*, 2001. Copyright © 2001 by the Royal Society of Medicine. Reproduced by permission.

its Declaration on the Human Genome and Human Rights, clearly human cloning arouses massive disapproval. What are the reasons, and especially the moral reasons, offered as justifications for this wholesale disapproval? In brief summary these seem to be: "yuk—the whole thing is revolting, repellent, unnatural and disgusting"; "it's playing God, hubris"; "it treats people as means and not as ends, undermines human dignity, human rights, personal autonomy, personality, individuality, and individual uniqueness; it turns people into carbon copies, photocopies, stencils, and fakes"; "it would be dangerous and harmful to those to whom it was done, as well as to their families: it would particularly harm the women who would be bearing the babies, and especially so if they were doing so on behalf of others as would probably be the case; it would harm societies in which it happened, changing and demeaning their values, encouraging vanity, narcissism, and avarice; and it would be harmful to future generations." "Altogether it would be the first massive step on a ghastly slippery slope toward"—here fill in the horror—Hitler's Nazi Germany, Stalin's USSR, China's eugenic dictatorship; or, from the realms of literature, *Boys from Brazil,* mad dictators, and of course mad scientists in science fiction, Big Brother in *Nineteen Eighty-Four,* and the human hatcheries of *Brave New World.*" "It would be unjust, contrary to human equality, and, as the European Parliament put it, it would lead to eugenics and racist selection of human beings, it would discriminate against women, it would undermine human rights, and it would be against distributive justice by diverting resources away from people who could derive proper and useful medical benefits from those resources." So, clearly, where it has not already been legally prohibited it should be banned as soon as possible.

Note that I have grouped these objections into five categories. The first constitute a highly emotionally charged group that includes yuk, horror, offence, disgust, unnaturalness, the playing of God, and hubris. Then come four clearly moral categories—those concerned with autonomy (in which for reasons given later I have included dignity); those concerned with harm; those concerned with benefit; and those concerned with justice of one sort or another, whether in the sense of simply treating people equally, of just allocation of inadequate resources, of just respect for people's rights, or in the sense of legal justice and the obeying of morally acceptable laws.

Types of Cloning

Two types of cloning have generated particular moral concern: the first involves taking a cell from a human embryo and growing it into a genetically identical embryo and beyond; the second, made famous by the creation of Dolly the sheep, involves taking out the nucleus of one cell and putting into the resulting sac, or cell wall, the nucleus of another cell to be cloned. Strictly, the Dolly-type clone is not quite a clone because the cell wall also contributes a few genes, the mitochondrial genes, which are incorporated into the resulting organism, but the vast majority of the genes in a Dolly-type clone come from the nucleus, so that, for example, if a nucleus from one of my cells were implanted into a cell sac from someone else, and the resulting cell were grown into a human being, he would have a gene complement almost but not entirely identical to mine. On the other hand, clones that result from splitting off of cells from embryos and growing them have exactly the same gene content as the embryo from which they came. With either of these cloning techniques, the process can be carried to early stages of development for a variety of potentially useful purposes, without any intention or prospect of producing a developed human being (lumped together here as nonreproductive human cloning and referred to only in passing). The human cloning that produces the greatest concern, and is the main subject of this [viewpoint], is of course reproductive human cloning, which would aim to produce a

human person with the same genes as some other human being.

The Gut Can't Be Trusted

First, then, the group of responses based on yuk, it's unnatural, it's against one's conscience, it's intuitively repellent, it's
playing God, it's hubris—a group of responses that one hears
very frequently. I have to admit that this sort of essentially
emotional response tends to evoke a negative emotional response in me when it is used in moral argument, as it often is
(by moral argument I mean, following David Raphael, argument about what is good or bad, what is right or wrong, what
ought or ought not to be done and about our values and
norms). The trouble is that these gut responses *may* be morally admirable, but they may also be morally wrong, even
morally atrocious, and on their own such gut responses do
not enable us to distinguish the admirable from the atrocious.
Think of the moral gut responses of your favorite bigots—for
example, the ones who feel so passionately that homosexuality
is evil, that black people are inferior, that women should be
subservient to men, that Jews and Gypsies and the mentally
retarded or mentally ill ought to be exterminated. People have
existed—some still exist—who have these strong "gut beliefs"
which they believe to be strong *moral* feelings, which indeed
they believe to be their consciences at work; and my point
here is that gut responses provide no way for us to distinguish
those moral feelings that we know or strongly believe to be
wrong, from the moral feelings that we ourselves have, which
we know or strongly believe to be right. To discriminate between emotional or gut responses, or indeed between the
promptings of deeply felt moral intuitions or of conscience,
we must reflect, think, analyze in order to decide whether particular moral feelings are good or bad, whether they should
lead to action or whether they should be suppressed (and yes,
I think moral reflection shows that it is important to suppress,

or even better reeducate so as to change, one's moral feelings when on analysis one finds they are wrong). Without such moral reflection the feeling itself, while it may be an important flag that warns us to look at the issues it concerns, is no more than that. With such reflection we may find that the flag is signaling an important moral perspective that we should follow: or we may find that the flag is signaling us to respond in a morally undesirable way.

An analogy which I like to use concerns medical practice. Doctors, especially surgeons, cut people up quite a lot: they (we) also stick their fingers in people's bottoms. Most of us, I imagine, would feel quite deeply that both of those activities are rather disgusting and not to be done, yet we know, through thought and reflection in our medical studies, that we had better overcome these deep feelings because in some circumstances it is right to cut people and in some circumstances it is right to put our fingers in people's bottoms. Both are extraordinary and counterintuitive things to do, but on analysis we find that they are sometimes the *right* thing to do. The same need for reflection, thought, and analysis applies to our deeply felt moral feelings in general. We need those deep moral feelings, those deep moral gut responses. Moral feelings are—here we may agree with [Scottish philosopher David] Hume—the mainsprings or drivers of our moral action. They lead us to action against social injustice and corruption, against the tyrant, the torturer, the sadist, the rapist, the sexual aggressor of children but—and now I part company with Hume—we need to reflect on and educate our moral feelings so as to select and develop the good ones, and deter and modify or preferably abolish the bad ones. . . .

Consider Twins

Certainly the existence of contemporary nature's own human clones, identical twins, seems harmless enough *not* to account for such deep hostility to the idea of deliberate cloning, though in passing it may be relevant to note that, down the ages, twins have been mysteriously subject to ambivalent prejudices. Thus, apart from literary and dramatic jokes about them from the comedies of Plautus via Shakespeare to Stephen Sondheim, twins and their mothers have been persecuted in some societies, revered but also feared in others, for example as unnatural miscogenated offspring of gods. On the other hand, there may be quite strongly positive attitudes to twins. Wendy Doniger in a review in the *London Bexlew of Books* quotes from Lawrence Wright's work on twins on "the common fantasy that any one of us might have a clone, a Doppel-ganger; someone who is not only a human mirror but also an ideal companion; someone who understands me perfectly, almost perfectly, because he is me, almost me."

We will return to the issue of identity, because the myth that genetic identity equals personal identity lies at the root of much misunderstanding about cloning. First, let us pursue in more detail the argument that cloning is *unnatural* and therefore wrong. What role does "unnatural" play in moral argument? Our first requirement is to disambiguate the term—what do we *mean* by unnatural in this context? Anything that occurs in nature could be said to be natural, but that sense of natural is not going to do much moral work for us, for we and what we do are natural, not unnatural, in this sense. In any case, right and wrong, good and bad, insofar as they occur in nature, also are equally natural in this sense, so that to say that something is natural will hardly help us distinguish between the two. Another sense of natural means unaffected by human intervention. But unless we wish to argue that all human interventions are bad and or wrong and all states of nature are good or right, then this sense of natural too is not much help for moral judgment. Think of all the truly horrible and morally undesirable things that occur in nature uninfluenced by humans; think too of all the human interventions in nature that are clearly morally desirable, but "unnatural" in this sense—including all medical interventions, and all the other activities by which we help each other, including the provision of food, housing, clothing, and heating.

Specific Reasons Needed

But there are two more senses of unnatural that are of moral relevance. The first is that it is part of human nature to be a moral agent (with perhaps a few exceptions) and thus human people who behave immorally or even amorally are acting unnaturally in this sense of acting against their human nature. I personally find this theme of enormous moral importance and a way of linking theological natural law theory with secular morality. But it does not afford us any simple basis or method for moral assessment—instead it demands assessment of what the moral part of our human nature requires of us. So "natural" in this sense, important though it is as a moral concept, does not give us a way of deciding whether cloning and the other genetics activities are good or bad—it simply requires us to make such distinctions. Like the objections based on the 'yuk response', the deep moral intuition, the moral repugnance and the claim of conscience, the objection that cloning is unnatural, when used in this morally plausible sense, requires moral reflection and judgment, but does not itself provide that moral reflection and judgment. If—but only if—such reflection and judgment lead us to conclude that cloning is immoral, *then* we can say that cloning is unnatural in this morally relevant sense of going against our moral nature.

There is another sense of unnatural which I think is also of potential moral relevance. If we do something that weakens, undermines, destroys, or harms our human moral nature, then this is immoral and unnatural in the sense of antinatural or against nature; and that of course is of enormous moral significance not just in relation to cloning but for the whole of the new genetics enterprise. So, to show that any activity, such as cloning, is unnatural in a morally relevant sense we need to give *reasons* that demonstrate why it is contrary to our human moral nature, or why it will undermine that human moral nature. Until we can give such reasons let us be particularly careful to avoid pejorative claims about cloning being unnatural, not simply for the reasons I have just given, but also because it must be very hurtful for the world's identical twins to hear that they, by association, are considered to be "unnatural" and therefore that their existence is morally undesirable. . . .

Personal Identity

The next set of objections against cloning concerns personal identity and dignity, the undermining of autonomy, of individuality, of personality, of uniqueness, the production of carbon copies, photocopies, stencils, and fakes of human beings.

Even if reproductive cloning were to produce a person identical with the person from whom he or she was cloned, it is not clear to me why this should be immediately condemned as morally unacceptable, though the idea so greatly strains the imagination that one might argue that it would be irresponsible to try any such trick even if it were possible. But of course reproductive cloning would *not* produce two identical people—only two people with identical (or in the case of Dolly-type cloning near identical) sets of genes. Genetic identity neither means nor entails personal identity. . . .

Some commentators make a different criticism. It is not only personal identity that must not be replicated; nor must genetic identity, for that itself is morally important, indeed even a right, according to the European Parliament. They assert that every one of us has a right to his or her own genetic identity. . . .

But if that is the European Parliament's claim it is not merely bizarre; if taken seriously it is morally malignant, for it implies morally malignant consequences for identical twins, nature's existing examples of people who are clones. If we have this right to genetic uniqueness, then somebody must have the corresponding duty—the duty to destroy one of each pair of existing identical twins, both born and *in utero*. Fortunately such counterexamples, plus the general tendency of morally reflective people to be morally and legally unconcerned about the lack of genetic uniqueness of identical twins, indicate that genetic uniqueness is unlikely, *pace* the European Parliament, to be of moral importance, let alone a moral right, and still less a right that ought to be enshrined in law. . . .

Human Dignity

Another objection to cloning that may also reside in the notion of human dignity is that we must never treat other people merely as means to an end, but always as ends in themselves—one of the versions of [Immanuel] Kant's categorical imperative. This claim is frequently misrepresented as a moral obligation never to use each other as means to an end, or as instruments or as tools or as objects. That misrepresentation is plainly wrong, for of course we morally can and morally do frequently use each other as means to an end, as tools, and it is highly desirable that we continue to do so. If I ask you to bend forward so that I can climb on your back in order to get over my garden wall to let myself in through the kitchen window because I have lost my key, I am using you as a means to my end, as an object, a sort of stepladder, an instrument or a tool. But I am not treating you *merely* as an object or a tool or an instrument. By asking and obtaining your permission I am treating you as an end in yourself as well as treating you as a means to my end. The issue is complicated with embryos because it is a matter of within the scope of the Kantian requirement to treat each other as ends in themselves. Many of us believe that they are not, and thus would permit, for example, the cloning of human embryos for research purposes with disposal (i.e., destruction) of the experimented-on embryo at an early stage in its development. In the United Kingdom the law allows this sort of thing. On the other hand, many others would say that this is morally outrageous because the human embryo *does* fall within the scope of the Kantian categorical imperative, being itself a human person from the moment of its creation. I am not going to address that argument, but it is important to see how it complicates the issue of cloning, both sorts of cloning. For if in creating an embryo, by whatever method, we have created a person, then of course we must treat it as a person, and thus not use it merely as a means to an end. If, on the other hand, it is not yet a person then we may use it merely as a means to an end, as a research tool for example, and destroy it after such use. That is an unresolved philosophical or theological problem.

Suppose, however, we put aside that piece of the argument and revert to human reproductive cloning. Then the requirement always to treat people as ends in themselves, even when we also treat them as means, is entirely compatible with reproductive cloning. The issue surely turns, not on the method of reproduction, cloning or otherwise, that one may choose, but rather on how one actually treats and regards the child that results. Take the example of parents who seek to clone a child because they want to have another child with the same blood or marrow type, so that they can transplant some marrow from the new child into an existing child mortally ill with leukemia. Such a process would necessarily involve, it is often claimed, treating the new child merely as a means. Not at all, I would counterargue. The argument needs to be broken down into two parts. The first part concerns the question, why do and ought people decide to have children? In particular, is there any moral obligation to have a child only for the sake of the child-to-be? If so, then surely the vast majority of parents have behaved immorally, for while there must be many different reasons for having a child, I doubt that there exist very many parents who have decided to have a child because they decided there was now a need to have a new person in the world to whom duties were owed that he or she should exist. Much more commonly (and yes, this is mere supposition) people decide to have a child because they *want* a child for their own reasons or, perhaps more commonly, instincts. They feel like it, or they are ready to have children, or they want to fill a gap in their lives, or perhaps they want an heir, or someone to take over the business, or someone to look after them in their old age; all sorts of personal selfish reasons may operate, or none at all. My argument is that, until shown otherwise, we should accept that there is nothing wrong with making either a self-interested or an instrumental decision to have a child.

Respect for the New Child

Having implemented such a decision, the second stage of the argument applies, for now of course mere self-interest can no longer be justified. Once there is another person created as a result of one's decision, then that person must be accorded the same moral respect as is due to all people and must not be treated merely as a means to an end, an object, a tool, an instrument. So while one may perfectly properly decide to have a child in order to provide a source of life-saving cord blood or marrow for one's existing child, one must of course then respect the new child as an end and never treat him or her merely as a means to an end. I can see no reason for the parents' instrumental motivation for having a child in any way necessitating their treatment of the new child merely as a means and not an end. If anything, I suspect that human psychological nature would tend to lead parents to treat such children even more lovingly and respectfully than usual.

I have given reasons for doubting that cloning would infringe the human dignity and autonomy of the cloned person. Let us now consider the dignity and autonomy of those who wish to engage in reproductive cloning. Such considerations favor noninterference on the grounds that in general people's autonomous choices for themselves should be respected, unless there are very strong moral reasons against doing so, and that this is particularly true in respect of those rather personal and private areas of choice, notably those concerning reproduction, sexuality, choice of partners, and decisions about babies. Intervention by the state, or anyone else, in these areas of private morality undermines the human dignity/autonomy of those people. Moreover, respect for people's dignity/autonomy in these areas is not only right in itself, but is also likely to lead to far greater overall good and far less harm than if we start erecting state apparatuses for intervention in these private areas. . . .

Better to Exist

What, then, of the formidable lists of harms, mainly psychological harms, anticipated to affect children? In brief, I think we need to set against these purported and anticipated psychological harms of being a clone child the very important counterconsideration of what is the alternative for that particular child? This argument commonly irritates, sometimes enrages, but rarely convinces. Yet it seems valid, and I have not encountered plausible *counterarguments*. The alternative *for those children* is to not exist at all, so if we are genuinely looking at the interests of those children who are anticipated to have the various psychological problems of being clones, and the difficulties that undoubtedly we can anticipate those will raise, and if we are genuinely looking at those problems from the point of view of the child, then the proper question to ask is: What is preferable for that child? To exist but to have those problems, or not to exist at all? It is an argument that I learned from the so-called pro-life movement, though I suspect this is not a use that pro-lifers themselves would wish to make of it. I found that the argument radically changed the way I thought about anticipated harms. Of course, it in no way stops one from deciding, for example, not to have a baby, or to have an abortion, or not to pursue reproductive cloning. But it does force one, or should force one, to realize that one's reasons are unlikely to be the best interests of the child whom one is thinking of not having, but are instead one's own reasons and preferences, largely about the sort of world one wishes to participate in creating. And if that is the case, why should one's own reasons and preferences prevail over the reasons and preferences of those who do wish to carry out reproductive cloning? After all, they do not claim a right to prevent us from reproducing according to our preferences; why should we claim a right to prevent them from reproducing according to their preferences?

As for the arguments about the potential social harms of cloning, other than those based on safety of the techniques, it seems to me that they are either frankly implausible (the argument that cloning is a threat to further human evolution surely falls into this category, given the likely numbers of cloned versus more conventionally produced people), too weak to justify imposition on those who reject them (for instance the arguments that reproductive cloning encourages vanity, narcissism, and avarice), or powerful but misdirected. Thus it is not cloning, nor the techniques of the new genetics more broadly considered, that might lead to the social harms of racism, eugenics, mass destruction, or the violation of the security of genetic material, but rather social structures that permit dictatorships and other forms of immorally enforced control of people's behavior by their rulers. Those are the harms that we need to be concerned about; and the most important way of avoiding them—of avoiding oppression of all those who are oppressed by the strong, including the widespread oppression of women by men—is not to ban cloning or to become obsessed with the new genetics, but rather to reform those social structures that result in such harms and to maintain in good order those social structures that do largely avoid these harms.

Concerns About the Germ Line

What about the germ-line argument of dangers to future generations? Well certainly the genome resulting from reproductive cloning is germ-line transmissible, and any mistakes that occur can be passed on to future generations. But so too, of course, can any benefits. If, for example, a cloning technique results in the elimination of some genetic abnormality that would otherwise have been transmitted through the germ line, then the cascade effect is geometrically beneficial, just as, if a mistake results and is passed on through the germ line, that, too, is geometrically inheritable. Clearly, care is needed to minimize the chances of the latter and maximize the chances of the former. But in general, with ever increasing voluntary personal control over reproduction, it seems likely that even if genetic mistakes do occur, if they are severe people will be reluctant to pass them on to their offspring, thus reducing the risks of a cascade of negative genetic effects down the generations. On the other hand the precedent of deciding to prevent certain sorts of reproduction on the basis of the risk to future generations of deleterious genetic effects is itself one of the social harms—enforced eugenics—that opponents of the new genetics are usually very keen to avoid.

Feminists Should Oppose Reproductive Technologies

Janice G. Raymond

Although there is a wide range of feminist views on assisted reproductive technologies (ART), in general, feminist intellectuals have responded to ART with suspicion. The following selection, from a book by feminist medical ethicist Janice G. Raymond, presents the view of feminists who are especially suspicious of reproductive technologies. Raymond argues that ART has not expanded women's reproductive choices but rather placed them in the hands of doctors and business owners. The people who actually benefit from reproductive technologies, she contends, are the predominately male medical professionals and fertility clinics. Raymond also contends that ART professionals dehumanize women by viewing them as egg repositories. Thus, she argues, reproductive technologies amount to a form of violence against women. Janice G. Raymond is a professor of women's studies and medical ethics at the University of Massachusetts, Amherst.

New reproductive arrangements are presented as a woman's private choice. But they are publicly sanctioned violence against women. The absoluteness of this privatized perspective, especially as emphasized by the medical profession and the media, who present women as having unconditioned free will, functions as a smoke screen for medical experimentation and, ultimately, for the violation of women's bodies. Choice so dominates the discourse that it is almost impossible to recognize the injury that is done to women.

Choice resonates as a quintessential U.S. value, set in the context of a social history that has gradually allowed all sorts of oppressive so-called options, such as prostitution, pornog-

Janice G. Raymond, *Women as Wombs: Reproductive Technologies and the Battle over Women's Freedom.* San Francisco: Harper, 1993. Copyright © 1993 by Janice G. Raymond. Reproduced by permission of the author.

raphy, and breast implants,to be defended in the name of women's right to choose. The language of choice is compelling because it highlights a freedom that many women seldom have and a cafeteria of options disguised as self-determination. Viewing reproductive technologies and contracts mainly as a woman's choice results from a particular Western ideology that emphasizes individual freedom and value neutrality. At the same time this ideology prevents us from examining technological and contractual reproduction as an institution and leads us to neglect the conditions that create industrialized breeding and the role that it plays in society. Choice so dominates the discussion that when critics of technological reproduction denounce the ways in which women are abused by these procedures, we are accused of making women into victims and, supposedly, of denying that women are capable of choice. To expose the victimization of women is to be blamed for creating women as victims.

Invisible Interests

Whose interests are served by representing technological reproduction as a woman's private choice while rendering invisible the force of institutionalized male-dominant interests? Furthermore, is choice the real issue, or is the issue *what* those choices are and in what context selective women's choices (surrogacy of IVF [in vitro fertilization]) are fostered? At the very least, choice implies awareness of possible consequences— what women lack in the reproductive technological and contractual context. At the very most, choice implies that women's health, autonomy, integrity, and basic social justice are served.

Various reproductive rights groups have included within their list of demands access to technological reproduction and surrogacy. Technological reproduction is sometimes defended as part of the pro-choice platform. Borrowing from the abortion defense, reproductive liberals contend that feminists must support these technologies and contracts as part of a woman's right to choose. The right to abortion is combined with the right to reproductive technologies and contracts as a total package that many women feel compelled to accept.

In the supposed interests of women, reproductive liberals have tried to silence critics of technological and contractual reproduction with the accusation that if we speak out against these procedures, we endanger women's reproductive freedom and give arguments to the anti-abortionists. Every criticism of these procedures is linked with the foes of abortion and subjected to the charges of stifling technology, freedom of research, and repressing women's choice. There is a vast difference, however, between women's right to choose safe, legal abortions and women's right to choose unsafe, experimental, and demeaning technologies and contracts. One allows genuine control over the course of a life; the other promotes abdication of control over the self, the body, and reproduction in general. Furthermore, our response to the right wing cannot simply be, "babies made to order." The concept of choice, if it is to have any feminist value, must not be advanced as an absolute right, else it risks reduction to a mere market consumerism.

Choice Subverted

The subverting of choice by the medical and corporate professionals to promote technological and contractual reproduction has been a largely unexamined area. The rhetoric of choice, however, belies its reality for women. Often what gets promoted as choice, such as the right to choose surrogate contracts, are outright constraints on women's capacity to choose. We cannot continue to pay lip service to reproductive choice while totally ignoring the control that these reproductive arrangements exercise over women. . . .

I contend that those who *support* and *promote* technological and contractual reproduction are *undermining* women's reproductive rights, especially women's right to abortion. The extent to which the rights of women are diminished when the fetus is part of the woman's body—for example, in conservative anti-abortion policy and legislation—should make us seriously question the extent to which they will be further diminished as the fetus is increasingly removed from the female body. Whether in the womb or outside, attention is riveted on the fetus as individual entity—patient, person, or experimentee. IVF; embryo experimentation, transfer, and freezing; and fetal tissue research sever the embryo/fetus from the woman. Reproductive technologies and contracts augment the rights of fetuses and would-be fathers while challenging the one right that women have historically retained some vestige of—mother-right.

We witness this assault on women's rights in surrogate custody disputes and in frozen embryo contests where the rights of "ejaculatory fathers" are presented as men's rights to gender equality (or, as the fathers' rights movement phrases it, "Equal rights are not for women only"). These techniques render women as spectators of rather than participants in the whole reproductive process. More and more, they reduce women to the status of vehicle for the fetus; biologically, they literally sunder the fetus from the pregnant woman. Politically and legally, technological reproduction tends to position the fetus as isolated and independent from the mother but not from the sperm source, the doctor, or the state.

The right to choose is fast becoming the right to consume. Reducing choice to consumption is nothing new. Corporate and professional interests, for many years, have used the rhetoric of choice to sell themselves and their products. What is new is the way in which liberalism and feminism have taken up the language of the corporate world and become consumer movements for new technologies and drugs—in the case of technological reproduction, for more and more dangerous and dubious technologies and drugs. The language of choice makes reproductive consumerism ethical.

This [viewpoint] is a challenge to reproductive liberalism, including its feminist variety. It is positioned against the liberal consumer movement that supports new reproductive technologies and contracts. It is not a balanced approach to both sides of the issue, nor does it provide the supporters of these technologies with equal time. Their position is dominant, well known, and widely publicized. Radical feminist work on the new reproductive technologies has effectively been censored in both the mainstream media and the mainstream feminist press. This [viewpoint] gives voice to these censored protests.

Reproductive Fundamentalism

Many people are willing to question a fundamentalism that is overtly religious, yet when these same practices appear in the guise of a secular science, they are not recognized as fundamentalism. Like other fundamentalisms, reproductive fundamentalism has a totalizing capacity. Psychiatrist Robert Jay Lifton has defined totalistic ideology as an exclusive claim to truth by full-blown manipulations of the environment. In analyzing "thought reform" in China, Lifton points to its ability to rehabilitate the individual by controlling specific but unlimited aspects of the person's environment. In *The Nazi Doctors,* Lifton applies this totalizing of the environment to what he calls "medical fundamentalism." I have used many of these totalizing features as a framework within which to view technological reproduction:

Milieu Control—Scientists and technologists shape public perception of the technologies through what social critics Edward Herman and Noam Chomsky call "manufacturing consent." Favorable press coverage of the technologies is created through a large public relations effort set up by hospitals and research facilities that are adept at marketing these technologies to the public through the media. Images of "miracle" technologies, drugs as "magic bullets," and society on the "frontier" of a "reproductive revolution" pervade the media presentation. Metaphors of progress dominate the coverage, and critical commentary is either ignored or confined to a capsulized space. Critics, who emphasize the political dimensions of medical research and technologies, tend to provide more in-depth analysis and are thus less likely to be quoted. Such critical commentary is not amenable to shrinkage—to the self-promoting sound bites of the scientific public relations enterprise that are so appealing to the media.

Mystical Manipulation—Clinicians represent themselves, and are represented, in the media as white-coated knights, altruistically seeking to help the infertile. "Help for the infertile" has been the dominant meaning given to these technologies. But infertility is a script—what the dictionary defines as a "dialogue spoken in a designated setting"—that was written *after* the technoscientists produced the technological scenario.

The script of infertility—the dialogue of benevolent doctors and desperate couples—came after the fact of technological reproduction, not before it. As Erwin Chargaff, a noted molecular biologist, has stated, "The demand [for the technologies] was less overwhelming than the desire on the part of the scientists to test their newly developed techniques. The experimental babies produced were more of a by-product." Chargaff's view is supported by reports that over 200,000 embryos have been stockpiled in European IVF centers that have been specifically created for research.

Sacred Science—Technological reproduction is mystified as the greatest hope for the infertile. Reproductive experts highlight successes and omit the numbers of failed attempts. The most blatant example of this misrepresentation is the reported IVF success rates in which success is often measured by the number of chemical pregnancies (hormone levels that may indicate pregnancy but are frequently false positives) and pregnancies per laparoscopy, many of which do not issue in live births. As surprising as this revelation has been to people, a large number of IVF clinics still do not measure success by numbers of live births. Many people do not know that the IVF success rate is between 0 percent and 15 percent, depending on the clinic, IVF success has been highest in Australia, yet a 1988 Australian government study found that "there is no evidence that IVF has had a higher success rate than other treatments for infertility, or even that it has a higher success rate than the absence of all treatment."

Loading of the Language—Medical and media claims that technological reproduction is a "cure for infertility" become a cliché that suppresses critical questioning. Unpacking this claim requires acknowledging that technological reproduction and surrogate contracts do not cure infertility but only provide some (mostly white, middle-class, married, heterosexual) couples with children and then, only a very small percentage of the time. Terms such as *surrogate mother* and *biological father* spawn new definitions of motherhood and fatherhood and stymie critical thinking about what the words mean. In the 1987 Baby M surrogacy case, the constant repetition of *surrogate mother* and *biological father,* like a mantra, helped confirm that Mary Beth Whitehead was a mere substitute rather than a real mother, while Bill Stern became the real parent rather than a sperm source. Stern's victory—being awarded custody of the child—was partly one of language. At other times, Stern was represented as simply the "father," and Whitehead as the "surrogate mother." She became the modified parent diminished by a qualifying adjective; his parenthood was straightforward—simply "father." The term *surrogate* reduces all women who sign surrogate contracts to incidental, nonparental status.

The new reproductive language is loaded in other ways. Are the deaths of women in IVF programs "unfortunate incidents" or "medical disasters"? Does it make a difference if Clomid, a hormone used to superovulate women on IVF programs to produce multiple eggs, is called a "potential risk" rather than a "debilitating drug"? Is the past history of reproductive drug and technology failures—as represented by thalidomide, diethylstilbestrol (DES), and estrogen replacement therapy, for example—"aberrant" or "typical"? Some words imply judgments; others convey value neutrality. Some trivialize an event; others highlight its significance. Choice of adjectives can marginalize some opinions while giving authority to others. Some words endow a technology with public stature; others diminish its status.

Doctrine over Person—Women's experiences of self, of reproduction, and of pregnancy are subsumed or negated by the system of technological reproduction. Women are not present in the medical language, which speaks only of "maternal environments" and "alternative reproductive vehicles." In the popular discourse about surrogacy, women who enter into surrogate arrangements have called themselves "baby-sitters" for "other people's children." Worse still, women are not present to themselves. One woman, passed along the in vitro fertilization production line, describes herself in the third person:

> Here she is . . . debased and degraded, embarrassed and humbled, shamed and subdued. Their guinea-pig, their hatching-hen, hormone cow, their willing victim. And why? Because, fifteen years ago, when all she willed was sex and not babies, the doctor put an IUD in her almost virgin womb.

Closely connected with the absence of self is *the dispensing of existence* experienced by women in technological reproduction. Time, relationships, jobs are dispensed with. Women undergoing these procedures report a sense of nonbeing:

> A broken vessel. A barren land. An empty shell. A nothingness, a nullity, a nonbeing.

This dispensing of existence is more than psychological and existential. Women on in vitro fertilization programs have literally died, and at least one woman lost her life while bearing a surrogate pregnancy from complications directly resulting from callous negligence of her heart condition by the broker—who was a real estate agent—and the doctor to whom she was sent.

As in other fundamentalisms, certain beliefs and principles are basic to the system of technological reproduction. The first principle is that *infertility is a disease for which reproductive technology is the remedy.* If doctors are curing a disease, then much becomes acceptable.

Sex Selection Will Lead to Global Instability

David Glenn

Now that reproductive technologies make sex selection increasingly easy, the preference of some Asian societies for sons may threaten global stability. That argument, presented by two scholars in a recent book, is critically examined in the following selection. According to writer David Glenn, the pair of scholars forecast that the growing surplus of sons in countries such as China and India will lead to increased violence and perhaps to war. Young men who cannot find wives are likely to be attracted to criminal gangs and militant groups, they argue. The researchers' case is built in part on the history of selective infanticide. The killing of female babies was commonplace at times in China's past, they observe. When the proportion of males swelled, violence and rebellion followed. Infanticide was then supplanted by selective abortion following tests that determine the sex of a fetus. As a result, there were about 20 percent more boys than girls in China in the early 1990s. However, Glenn reports that the scholars' argument that surplus sons will lead to instability fails to persuade some historians. Skeptics charge that the researchers' evidence has been selectively presented to favor their argument. David Glenn is a correspondent for the Chronicle of Higher Education.

A body of Chinese poetry, *The Book of Songs*, believed to date from 1000–700 B.C., offers this advice to new parents:

When a son is born,

Let him sleep on the bed,

David Glenn, "A Dangerous Surplus of Sons?" *The Chronicle of Higher Education*, vol. 50, April 30, 2004, pp. A14–18. Copyright © 2004 by *The Chronicle of Higher Education*. This article may not be published, reposted, or redistributed without express permission from *The Chronicle*.

Clothe him with fine clothes,
And give him jade to play with. . . .

When a daughter is born,
Let her sleep on the ground,
Wrap her in common wrappings,
And give her broken tiles for play-
things.

In many parts of Asia, that advice appears to have stuck. Centuries later, a strong preference for sons persists, enhanced by technology that increasingly allows parents to real-
ize their desires. Amniocentesis and ultrasound can easily
identify the sex of a fetus, end sex-selective abortion has become an everyday practice. Daughters who are born are frequently given up, and thousands are adopted out of the country every year. On the horizon are inexpensive sperm-sorting
techniques that will guarantee a son even before conception.
New technology, of course, is not the only factor; in some rural areas, old-fashioned female infanticide still lingers.

The reasons for the persistence of offspring sex selection,
and the exact numbers of pregnancies involved, have been
hotly debated since the early 1990s, when the economist Ama-
rtya Sen called attention to the phenomenon of "missing
women." By some social scientists' measure, more than 100
million females are now missing from the populations of India and China. Mr. Sen and others have argued that sex selection both reflects and reinforces women's low social status,
which—beyond its intrinsic cruelty—impedes the development of democracy and prosperity in male-skewed nations.
Scholars and feminist organizations in both Asia and the West
have produced many volumes of often conflicting advice about
how to combat the practice.

Now two political scientists have joined the fray with an
ominous argument: Offspring sex selection could soon lead to
war.

In a new book, *Bare Branches: Security Implications of Asia's Surplus Male Population,* Valerie M. Hudson and Andrea M. den Boer warn that the spread of sex selection is giving rise to a generation of restless young men who will not find mates. History, biology, and sociology all suggest that these "surplus males" will generate high levels of crime and social disorder, the authors say. Even worse, they continue, is the possibility that the governments of India and China will build up huge armies in order to provide a safety valve for the young men's aggressive energies.

The Outlet of War

"In 2020 it may seem to China that it would be worth it to have a very bloody battle in which a lot of their young men could die in some glorious cause," says Ms. Hudson, a professor of political science at Brigham Young University.

Those apocalyptic forecasts garnered a great deal of attention when the scholars first presented them, in the journal *International Security,* in 2002. "The thing that excites me about this research is how fundamental demography is," says David T. Courtwright, a professor of history at the University of North Florida and author of *Violent Land: Single Men and Social Disorder from the Frontier to the Inner City,* a study of sex ratios and murder rates in American history. "The basic idea that they have, that in some sense demography is social destiny—that's a very powerful idea."

But other experts are unpersuaded. They say that Ms. Hudson and Ms. den Boer's argument rests too heavily on a few isolated historical cases, and that the authors have failed to establish a systematic correlation between sex ratios and violence. Critics also suggest that the argument promotes false stereotypes of men and masculinity, and that the authors do not offer detailed knowledge of Asian societies and political systems. Offspring sex selection is indeed a serious problem, the critics say, but to treat it as a problem of international security is an unwarranted distraction.

The two political scientists began their project in the mid-1990s, when Ms. den Boer—who is now a lecturer in international politics at the University of Kent, in England—was a graduate student at Brigham Young. Ms. Hudson regularly assigned the philosopher Daniel Little's book *Understanding Peasant China: Case Studies in the Philosophy of Social Science,* which mentions that 19th-century Chinese rebellions were concentrated in areas that were disproportionately male.

Intrigued by that insight, Ms. Hudson and Ms. den Boer began to search for similar patterns elsewhere. "It was sort of random research at the beginning," says Ms. den Boer. "Where has female-selective infanticide been prevalent in the past? Then we looked at where the practice is prevalent today . . . and then looked further at the correlations with violence."

"I don't think we initially set out to write a book," she continues. "We initially, in fact, just wrote a conference paper. There was a lot of interest in that paper. The CIA came to the university and spoke with us about it, and wanted to know what United States policy should be toward countries that have this prevalence of infanticide and high sex ratios." (In demographers' jargon, a "high-sex-ratio" society is male-skewed, and a "low-sex-ratio" society is disproportionately female. The worldwide sex ratio is estimated to be 101, meaning that there are 101 men for every 100 women.)

Bare Branches offers some disheartening numbers: In 1993 and 1994, more than 121 boys were born in China for every 100 baby girls. (The normal ratio at birth is around 105; for reasons debated among biologists, humans seem naturally to chum out slightly more boys than girls.) In India during the period 1996 to 1998, the birth ratio was 111 to 100; in Taiwan in 2000, it was 109.5. In 1990 a town near New Delhi reported a sex ratio at birth of 156.

Unyielding Desire for Sons

Scholars have offered a number of explanations for the remarkable persistence of son-preference, which has lingered even in regions confronted by modernizing forces and government efforts to stamp out female infanticide. A powerful Chinese social norm, especially strong in rural areas, holds that sons must care for their parents in old age; people without sons thus fear poverty and neglect. In both India and China, various folk beliefs hold that only a son can perform the religious rituals that will ease a deceased parent's way into the afterlife.

Some scholars suggest that those norms and beliefs are remnants of a long-ago time when there were narrowly rational reasons to prefer sons to daughters. Anthropological studies have found, for example, that female infanticide and son-worship sometimes emerge in warring nomadic communities that frequently lose many men in battle, or that are vulnerable to having their women and children kidnapped by a rival group. In such situations, the theory goes, a group can preserve its integrity by tightly controlling the number of women within it.

Another theory holds that son-preference is a by-product of hypergyny, a system in which women are expected to marry men of higher social rank. Strongly hypergynous societies tend to have dowry rituals; the bride's family gives money to the groom's family as an emblem of the bride's subordinate status. (A Chinese truism says: "The family of the married daughter holds its head down, while the family of the man whom she has married holds its head up.") The great cost and social shame long associated with dowries can make parents cringe at the thought of having a new daughter.

Americans often assume that hypergyny and a preference for sons must be self-correcting, according to Ms. Hudson. As marriageable daughters become scarce, people will choose to produce more of them. Simple supply and demand, right?

"If there's an economist in the audience," the professor says, "he or she will raise this point: 'When you make something scarce, you'll make it more valuable—this will improve the social position of women.' And it's just utterly false.... It doesn't take account of the fact that the woman herself does not hold her value. That is, she herself could not use her scarcity to improve her condition, because her fate is determined by men, either her father or her husband's family. She herself cannot leverage her scarcity."

"There's also a sort of NIMBY phenomenon that goes on here," Ms. Hudson continues, alluding to the "not in my backyard" attitude. "Individual fathers and families will say, Yes, it's important that girls be born, that there be wives for our sons. But I want a son! We'll let somebody else have the girls."

Impending Crisis

Whatever the causes of sex selection, Ms. Hudson and Ms. den Boer are certain that it threatens the stability of eastern Asia.

"We're right on the cusp," says Ms. Hudson. By that she means that birth ratios began to skew around 1985, as sex-selection technology spread, and that the "surplus" boys born in the late 1980s are just now reaching adulthood. "With every passing year, these surplus males will become more and more an important social factor." She cites news reports of spikes in drinking, gambling, and violent crime among young men in rural Indian villages.

As their ranks grow, these unmarried young men are likely to be attracted to militant organizations, the authors say. In such an "unstable context," they write, the conflicts over Taiwan and Kashmir, for example, are unlikely to be permanently settled. What's more, the governments of Asian nations may cope with the social strains caused by their "bare branches"—a Chinese term for men who cannot find spouses—by turning to militarism and ultranationalism.

"The security logic of high-sex-ratio societies predisposes nations to see some utility in interstate conflict," the authors write. In addition to stimulating a steadier allegiance from bare branches, who are especially motivated by issues involving national pride and martial prowess, conflict is often an effective mechanism by which governments can send bare branches away from national population centers, possibly never to return."

The authors rest their case in part on historical case studies. Female infanticide was rampant in 18th-century China, and the Qing dynasty responded by encouraging single men to colonize Taiwan, they write. As a result, Taiwan developed an extremely high sex ratio and soon was swept by groups that combined banditry with anti-imperial rebellion. The "Heaven and Earth Society" became so powerful that in 1787 the government was forced to send thousands of troops to restore order.

A similar story had unfolded in 16th-century Portugal, where primogeniture was in practice. Because first-born sons inherited everything, many later-born sons had no chance of finding wives. According to James L. Boone, a University of New Mexico anthropologist, such later-born sons banded together to persuade the monarch to launch wars of conquest in Africa. "It was above all the cadets," Mr. Boone wrote, "who lacked land and other sources of revenue within the country, who desired war, which would permit them to accede to a position of social and material independence."

Ms. Hudson and Ms. den Boer also point to a series of empirical tests—including one they have conducted themselves—demonstrating a positive correlation between sex ratios and murder rates across India.

Critics Call for Evidence

Nothing in the two women's arguments, however, persuades Joshua S. Goldstein, a professor emeritus of international relations at George Washington University, who wrote *War and Gender: How Gender Shapes the War System and Vice Versa.* "The problem with their design is that they're basically just picking cases that fit their hypothesis, and so you don't know whether it's generalizable or not," he says. Mr. Goldstein would prefer a much more systematic study, one that would try to identify how sex ratios interact with other variables that are believed to be linked to instability and war: rapid population growth, ethnic tension, poverty, and unstable availability of resources.

Melvin Ember agrees. "Arguing by example is not anywhere near truth or confirmation," says Mr. Ember, president of the Human Relations Area Files, a repository of anthropological data at Yale University. "A better study would look at a large, randomly selected sample of societies with high, low, and normal sex ratios," he says. "It just requires a little bit of good will and money. The statistical techniques and the databases exist."

A similar complaint is offered by Manju Parikh, an associate professor of political science at the College of St. Benedict, who has written about offspring sex selection. "This is an example of social-science inductive reasoning, but it's not a very good example," she says. "They have to show why other explanations don't do as well. This is not a unique situation"—that is, she says, many countries with normal sex ratios have also been prone to instability and war.

Those complaints reflect a too-rigid model of explaining the world, responds Ms. Hudson, who teaches courses in social-science methodology. "This critique goes to the heart of how we know anything in the social sciences," she says, arguing that because skewed sex ratios are a still-emerging variable, it is appropriate to sketch their potential effects more loosely, using what she and Ms. den Boer call "confirmatory process tracing."

"I encourage others who wish to perform additional analysis using other methods to do so," Ms. Hudson says. "But until a question is even raised, it cannot be addressed."

Mr. Goldstein and Ms. Parikh also worry that the *Bare Branches* argument leans too heavily on what they regard as crude evolutionary models of male behavior. "The authors seem to completely lack empathy for these low-status rootless men," says Ms. Parikh. "These guys are the victims of development, and they call them criminals and potential criminals. This is so appalling." For instance, contrary to the book's suggestion, she says, most migrant workers in Asia maintain strong kinship ties with their home villages, send money home every month, and are nothing like the untethered marauders pictured in the authors' warnings.

The term "surplus males," Mr. Goldstein says, "is offensive, and for lack of a better term, sexist. They're making a very conservative argument, which is sort of wrapped up in a feminist skin." It is a mistake, he says, to draw easy lessons from the finding that unmarried men tend to have higher testosterone levels than do their married peers.

Ms. Hudson says she herself is skeptical of sociobiological explanations but finds it impossible to avoid engagement with them. "I don't know of any social-science findings that are more confirmed than the fact that young men monopolize violent antisocial behavior in every society," she says. "It may not be PC to say so, but you come up against such a mountain of evidence."

As for Ms. Parikh's point about migrant workers' kinship ties, Ms. Hudson says that "feeling kinship with home and village is not the point. . . . Even when bare branches stay close to home, when they congregate they form new systems of norms unto themselves." Those new norms are often aggressive and antisocial, she says. "Families cannot control their 'stakeless' sons."

Mr. Courtwright, of North Florida, agrees. His 1996 book argues that violent crime in the United States has been concentrated in areas with high sex ratios, like the old Western frontier, and areas with low sex ratios, like contemporary urban ghettos, from which significant numbers of men are "missing" because of imprisonment. Such demographic considerations should be central to any serious study of crime and disorder, he says. "Even if you don't buy their fears about war," he says of Ms. Hudson and Ms. den Boer, "certainly you can accept their predictions about crime and instability."

The argument presented in *Bare Branches* is akin to one developed in the late 1990s by the Canadian psychologists Neil I. Wiener and Christian G. Mesquida. They argued that violence and conflict are tightly correlated with a given society's "male age ratio," the ratio of men age 15 to 29 to men age 30 and older. If there is a relatively high proportion of young men, they say, a society is much more prone to violence. In Mr. Wiener and Mr. Mesquida's framework, young men are hard-wired for "coalitional aggression" as they fight for resources and potential mates.

The upshot of that argument is optimistic: The two psychologists predict that war and conflict will diminish during the 21st century, as the world's median age rises and the male age ratio improves. (Mr. Goldstein finds their optimism comically overdrawn, noting that the York University alumni magazine has quoted Mr. Mesquida as flatly declaring, "Right now we don't have to worry about Russia because their population is static.")

Mr. Wiener is enthusiastic about Ms. Hudson and Ms. den Boer's work, and says they are asking exactly the right questions about Asia's future. "Males cause trouble," he says. The prospect of tens of millions of unmarried men "is potentially extremely disruptive for these societies."

Predictions Disputed

No matter how disruptive such men might be, skeptics say, Ms. Hudson and Ms. den Boer cannot make accurate predictions about the effects because they are insufficiently familiar with the details of Asian political systems and social life. "The political leadership in China has been heavily held in place for the last 25 years by the fact that they have kept the country out of war," says Mr. Goldstein, who finds it implausible that the regime would increase its militarism simply in order to soak up free-floating bachelors. "In any case, the kinds of wars that are fought these days don't involve human waves of 20 million unmarried men," he says.

As for a rise in Chinese nationalism, he says, that is indeed a concern, but it has little to do with bands of low-status bare branches, as Ms. Hudson and Ms. den Boer write. "It's not unmarried men out in mining camps who are whipping this up," Mr. Goldstein says. "It's college students and young professionals on the Internet chat rooms and such. So they really didn't convince me at all that these bare branches would be a source of any change in foreign policy."

Ms. Hudson concedes that her conjectures about foreign-policy changes are speculative—necessarily so, she says, because the first bare branches are only now reaching adulthood. But she insists that her speculations are plausible and urgent: "To think about such things before they might happen is an important part of reducing the probability of unwanted consequences."

Partly in response to feminist activism, Asian governments have taken steps to curb sex selection. India now bans public hospitals from performing sex-determination ultrasound tests (though the ban is nearly impossible to enforce), and at least three Indian states have outlawed sex-selective abortions. In 1996 China posted propaganda billboards featuring two older women. One, who appears destitute, says, "I have three sons, but none of them takes care of me." The other, who is comfortably dressed, replies, "I have only one daughter, but she surpasses your three sons." (The daughter appears on the billboard, rubbing her mother's back.)

Such efforts have had limited effects. [In March 2004] Khalid Malik, the U.N. resident coordinator in China, issued a statement warning that if present birth rates continue, as many as 60 million more women could be "missing" from China's population within 10 years.

"People are exercising their preferences," he told reporters. "But the consequences for society are enormous."

The High Costs and Health Risks of Reproductive Technologies

Kelly Kershner

Reproductive technology has fulfilled the hopes of some infertile people, but it has also blighted the hopes of others. In the following selection Kelly Kershner examines the question of whether in vitro fertilization (IVF) is worth the risks and costs associated with it. Kershner cites the arguments of critics who say that the $2 billion a year spent on reproductive treatments such as IVF divert funds from other medical needs. Moreover, critics say, assisted reproduction technology and the market-driven industry that has grown up around it are undermining adoption, which can meet the needs of infertile individuals and children in need of parents. In addition, women undergoing IVF can suffer pain due to complications, and couples experience intense emotional distress when such procedures fail. Kelly Kershner writes on health and medical issues for numerous publications, including USA Today.

Jaime Romano knew something was wrong. She'd had gynecological problems since she was 18 and had seen several doctors over the last 12 years about recurrent abdominal pain and abnormal vaginal bleeding—mostly without success. This time, though, it was different. "One of my Fallopian tubes had wrapped itself around my ovary, which became cystic and burst. I had developed such a high tolerance for pain that, by the time they operated, my abdominal cavity was full of gangrene."

"Since I was in my early 20s, I'd had a feeling that pregnancy was something that would not come easily. After my surgery, I realized that in-vitro fertilization [IVF] would be my only option."

Two years later, Romano and her husband, Frank, decided to try it. Jaime began taking a series of hormone injections to boost her functioning ovary's egg production. For about a week, she endured almost-daily blood tests and ultrasounds—measures fertility specialists use to gauge when eggs are mature enough for removal. Finally, it was time. The Romanos' fertility specialist retrieved Jaime's ripe eggs and mixed them in a special solution with Frank's sperm. A day or so later, fertilization occurred; tiny embryos began to divide and grow—two cells, then four. A day later, the fertility specialist transferred four of these microscopic clusters of cells into Jaime's uterus. Everyone hoped for the best. It didn't work. About a year later, the Romanos tried IVF again, without success.

Bitter Losses

Today [1996], Jaime Romano feels some bitterness about the costs and pitfalls of IVF. "My husband and I have spent more than $20,000 pursuing IVF. The cost has affected everything we do—our savings, our vacations, work on our house. It's always near the surface of our existence. If we are not discussing it, then one of us is thinking about it. Plus, it seems that many clinics are now emphasizing marketing. They are twisting numbers and misleading patients—patients who are vulnerable and desperate and can be easily led down the primrose path. I'll just say this—the doctor who performed our second IVF is held in very low esteem in our household."

Despite these concerns, the Romanos have not given up. "We'll be giving IVF another try. . . . I've wanted to have a child since I myself was a child. I feel I should pursue the options this technology gives me."

Jaime Romano's mixed feelings about IVF are not surprising. By any measure, assisted reproductive technologies are amazing medical breakthroughs. For the fortunate few, they are remedies for the heartbreak of infertility. Nevertheless, there are pitfalls, including high cost, pain, vulnerability to deception, and dashed dreams. There also are the larger societal questions about these technologies' worth: What are the true costs and benefits for individuals and society? How do these technologies affect women's and infants' health? Do they exploit women? Empower them? Are they anti-adoption? Is the possibility of conceiving a biological child worth any price?

Costly and Chancy

Assisted reproductive technologies are expensive. The costs are high: a single IVF attempt runs an average of $8,000; one GIFT (gamete intrafallopian transfer, in which retrieved eggs and sperm are mixed and transferred to the Fallopian tube) attempt is even more—an average of $10,000. Moreover, the costs are not limited to a single attempt. A 1994 *New England Journal of Medicine* study found that the expense of a successful delivery with IVF ranges from $67,000 (if a child is conceived on the first attempt) to almost $115,000 (if it takes six attempts). For couples where the woman is over 40 and the man has a low sperm count, it ranges from $160,000 to $800,000.

What's more, these technologies offer fairly slim chances of success. According to the Society for Reproductive Medicine, the odds that a single ovarian stimulation cycle—the beginning point of assisted reproductive technologies—will result in a live birth are about 14%. The odds with GIFT are a bit better—22%. However, these figures are averages for both younger and older women. Computed separately, a 40-plus woman's chances of having a baby through IVF are about three–five percent; with GIFT, nine percent.

Some health organizations have taken these figures to heart, arguing that assisted reproductive technologies result in few proven benefits. In 1990, the World Health Organization issued a summary report defining IVF as experimental, contending that, because IVF has not undergone a thorough and careful scientific evaluation, it should not be presented as a standard medical practice. In 1993, after a three-year study of infertility treatments, the Canadian Royal Commission on Reproductive Technologies concluded that IVF can be considered a proven treatment for only one type of infertility—blocked Fallopian tubes.

Not surprisingly, women who've given birth to a child through assisted reproductive technologies have much different views. "The costs have been worth it—most definitely," maintains Barbara Merton, a bank manager in her early 30s. She and her husband, Daryl, spent five years and $4,000 seeing infertility specialists, then she became pregnant the month after stopping treatment. "Some of the drug therapies had to have helped do something," she says. "I don't think it was all for naught."

Merton is not alone. When it comes to assisted reproductive technology, people are willing to shell out considerable amounts for even the slimmest chance of success. In a 1992 study, scientists asked 150 people how much they'd be willing to pay for a 10% chance at having a child through IVF, should they find themselves infertile. The average answer was $17,730.

Costs to Society

Of course, each person has his or her own notions of acceptable costs and benefits. As Elizabeth Bartholet, a Harvard University law professor who pursued high-tech fertility treatment before opting for adoption, pointed out in *Family Bonds: Adoption and the Politics of Parenting:* "Those who produce a child will say it has all been worth it. [But] a quick assessment of the costs and benefits of IVF raises serious questions about whether this new method for dealing with infertility should be seen as a net plus for women, for children or for the larger society. For the society at large, it is the total cost of IVF that is relevant. These resources could be devoted to serving some of the most basic health care needs of women and children, which now go unmet."

Janice Raymond, a professor of women's studies and medical ethics at the University of Massachusetts at Amherst, echoes this sentiment in *Women as Wombs: Reproductive Technologies and the Battle over Women's Freedom:* "Some will say that these reproductive technologies need not be pitted against access to basic health needs. Yet these technologies can only be defended in the interests of servicing the few, not the many others whose pressing needs go unmet because research and money are siphoned off in the quest for more profitable and high technologies of reproduction."

For some, these arguments are compelling. The $2,000,000,000 spent on fertility treatment in the U.S. each year, they insist, could be better spent on prenatal care, efforts to lower infant mortality, and vaccinations for children already born. Others, though, don't subscribe to this way of thinking.

"It's true that things like IVF do not result in good accruing equally to everyone," indicates Bernard Rosen, associate professor of philosophy, Ohio State University. "But certainly the total amount of good in the world goes up as a result of these technologies. As for the argument that we could be doing different things with the money spent on IVF, that's based on the assumption that there's some way to get the money and transfer it to other purposes. Given the political and economic systems we have, that is not going to happen."

Medical Considerations

Perhaps a more important thing to consider with these technologies is the medical risks and complications associated with ovary-stimulating drugs in general—especially Pergonal injections. "With Pergonal, ovarian hyperstimulation is the rule, rather than the exception," explains Moon Kim, a fertility specialist and professor of obstetrics and gynecology at Ohio State University. "The ovaries become large because they have produced so many eggs. When that happens, a woman can experience nausea, pain, fluid collecting in the abdomen, twisted ovaries—all kinds of problems can occur. However, because of careful monitoring, probably fewer than one percent of these women end up in the hospital."

As for IVF in particular, studies have linked it to increased risk of infection, pregnancy-induced high blood pressure, first trimester bleeding, and—most alarming—increased miscarriage. "With IVF, even in younger women, the miscarriage rate is higher than it is naturally, about 20%," notes Kim. Statistics bear this out. In 1992, for instance, 20% of the IVF and 21.5% of GIFT attempts in the U.S. ended in miscarriage.

Assisted reproductive technologies also can have adverse health effects on the infants they help produce. Take the case of IVF. To increase the odds of success, many couples and their fertility specialists decide to have three or more embryos transferred to the woman's uterus. This leads to a higher-than-normal number of multiple pregnancies. About one in three of the pregnancies achieved through IVF and GIFT result in multiple births.

That is where the problems begin. Twins, triplets, and other multiples are about 10 times more likely to be born prematurely and at low birth weight. These small, premature infants, in turn, are at increased risk of neurological and sensory disabilities and death in the first month of life. An Australian study, for instance, found that the first-month death rate for IVF babies was four times that of the normal population.

"The media treats multiple births with the hype usually reserved for celebrities," Kim indicates. "But I think that is the wrong message. Multiple births are a serious complication. Most of the babies survive, but there are increased incidences of neurological problems later on in life."

The medical risks of assisted reproductive technologies are clear, though some argue that not providing these services for couples who desperately want children has dangers of its own. Among infertile women, the risk of long-term psychological damage is real. Studies show that the infertile suffer twice the instances of major depression as other women. A 1993 study at Harvard Medical School found that the anxiety and depression experienced by infertile women was similar to that of females with heart disease, cancer, and HIV-positive status.

"Being infertile destroyed my self-image, my confidence," says Barbara Merton. "I felt like I had no control. I got to the point that I didn't want to get up in the morning. I'd get a 'guess what, I'm pregnant' call from a friend, and I'd just start sobbing, I'd cry for hours over things like that."

As a "treatment" for this sort of depression, assisted reproductive technology can be a cure that works. A 1994 study found that infertile women who become parents experience greater well-being. Nevertheless, it's a risky course of action—an all-or-nothing option. When assisted reproductive technology is unsuccessful, it actually can make things worse.

Many Failures

"IVF is a numbers game," maintains Elizabeth Bartholet. "The chances of succeeding are always low on any attempt, so it is easy to experience any given failure not as a reason to stop, but as a reason to keep going. When you have invested so much, it can seem silly to stop." Burdened by their expectations, she says, "unsuccessful" infertile couples become trapped in an almost unbearable cycle of hope and despair, month after month. Within even one IVF cycle, each of the stages becomes a grand victory—or a dismal defeat. A *New York Times* writer put it well: "IVF didn't invent the sorrow of infertility. But it has certainly added a uniquely perverse dimension to that pain."

Advocates of assisted reproductive technology concede these points. They agree that IVF and its high-tech cousins can be painful, both physically and mentally. However, they are quick to add, infertile women elect to participate in these technologies knowing the risks. The pain is the price infertile women choose to pay for expanded reproductive choices.

"These technologies offer reproductive opportunities for women," explains Rosen. "There is some harm to women involved, but this is harm that is self-inflicted, voluntarily chosen. It would be paternalistic to close these technologies down and bar access to them under the auspices of protecting women from themselves. We act paternalistically with children because they don't know what's good for them. That's not the case here. Women understand what's involved and choose to proceed anyway."

Choice or Coercion?

Critics of assisted reproductive technologies see things differently. The expanded reproductive choice these technologies claim to offer, they maintain, is not really choice at all—it's coercion. They argue that, in American society, females who are childless are stigmatized as selfish and uncaring careerists, aberrant radicals uncommitted to family values and maternal ideals. Given this political context, an infertile woman has limited choices: try high-tech treatment until it works or the money runs out, or be dubbed a social misfit. For most, the "choice" is clear. They submit to treatment.

"In a culture that so thoroughly defines a woman's identity in terms of motherhood, the fact that women agree to participate in IVF programs does not mean they are truly free not to participate," Paul Lauritzen wrote in his essay, "What Price Parenthood?" "The problem here might reasonably be called the tyranny of available technologies. If the technology exists, the expectation is that it will be used."

In *Women as Wombs,* Janice Raymond takes this argument even further. She states that not only are assisted reproductive technologies coercive, they're also blatantly sexist. "When technological reproduction perpetuates the role of women as breeders or encourages women to have children at any cost, this is not reproductive self-determination. It is conformity to old social roles garbed in new technologies and the new language of individual rights and choice. A woman's life, work and health are demoted when they do not mesh with her reproductive worth."

Bartholet also has ethical problems with assisted reproductive technologies. She maintains that infertile couples are driven away from adoption and toward fertility treatment by both physicians and the larger society. As a result, infertile couples try IVF for too long and thus lose the opportunity or will to be adoptive parents. Perhaps even more heartbreaking, parentless children lose the chance to be adopted into loving homes.

Stigma Around Adoption

"The specialized fertility experts in today's treatment world have little interest in or knowledge about adoption," she claims in *Family Bonds.* "Also, adoption has a very bad name. The stigma surrounding it is so pervasive that most people are unaware of its existence, it is part of the air we breathe, part of the atmosphere of our daily existence. The infertile are bombarded with messages that reinforce the idea that it makes sense to consider adoption, if at all, only as a last resort."

As evidence of this bias, Bartholet cites the countless overwrought media stories about adoptees and their "real families" being "reunited." A recent study by a media scholar, in fact, found that one-third of all news stories on adoption deal with birth parents who are searching for or reclaiming their children.

Bartholet places some blame for anti-adoption bias on adoption agencies themselves. "The adoption world does essentially nothing to reach out to the infertile to educate them about adoption possibilities. [Agencies] drive people away from adoption by surrounding it with burdensome regulations and by artificially limiting the number of children available out of all those desperately in need of homes."

In fairness, though, adoption agencies are not entirely to blame. The supply of American infants available for adoption has fallen off dramatically in recent years. Currently, fewer than one percent of the infants born in the U.S. each year are placed for adoption. Of those born to unmarried teenagers or women, just two percent are placed for adoption—down from nearly 10% 15 years ago.

So what is the bottom line on assisted reproductive technology? The issues surrounding it are significant. The price of high-tech treatments is higher than some can or should pay. Medically and psychologically, these treatments have risks that can't be ignored. Were this an ideal world, adoption would fulfill the hopes and dreams of childless couples. Yet, biases exist, adoption is an imperfect solution to infertility, and babies are hard to come by. Reaching consensus on assisted reproductive technology is difficult; clear-cut answers remain elusive.

Chronology

1825 B.C.

Ancient Egyptian physicians compose the so-called Kahun Gynecology Papyrus, in which they describe various ways to treat women, including using garlic to diagnose infertility.

ca. 1200

Statues of Ramses II, a pharaoh who had many children, are erected at the ancient Egyptian city of Tanis and later become fertility shrines.

A.D. ca. 1260

Citing Genesis 30:14, the medieval Jewish physician and rabbi known as Nachmanides recommends herbal remedies for infertility.

1651

Physician William Harvey, rejecting earlier ideas about human development, argues that each individual develops step by step in the fertilized egg. This becomes known as the theory of epigenesis.

1677

Dutch microscope pioneer Anton Van Leeuwenhoek discovers sperm in male ejaculate.

1779

British doctor James Graham opens an infertility business based on what he calls "electro-therapy." After a five-year run of commercial success, he is denounced as a fraud and his business declines.

1784

Using a dog, Italian scientist Lazzaro Spallanzani performs the first successful artificial insemination, resulting in the birth of three pups.

1785

Scottish surgeon John Hunter makes the first known attempts at human artificial insemination.

ca. 1850

American surgeon J. Marion Sims develops the first speculum and later performs the first cervical surgeries aimed at repairing infertility. He becomes known as the father of gynecology.

1901

German embryologist Hans Spemann performs the first known cloning experiment. By splitting a two-cell newt embryo, he causes two genetically identical newts to be born from one conception.

1913

A University of Chicago professor of surgery performs the first successful human testicle transplant, on a thirty-three-year-old man.

1914

Spemann conducts an early embryology experiment that lays the groundwork for cloning by somatic nuclear transfer.

1920

Researcher I.C. Rubin publishes an article about his newly developed test for blocked fallopian tubes, a major cause of female infertility, in the *Journal of the American Medical Association.*

1923

Physiologist Edgar Allen and biochemist Edward A. Doisy discover the female reproductive hormone estrogen.

1931

German researcher Adolf Butenandt discovers the male sex hormone, which he names androsterone. It is later renamed testosterone.

1943

Synthetic hormone supplements become available.

1944

Harvard physician John Rock and his colleagues fertilize four human eggs in a laboratory dish, the first known instance of in vitro fertilization (IVF). The embryos are not implanted.

1949

Christopher Polge reports success in freezing animal semen for future use in artificial insemination.

1960

Ovarian stimulation drugs Clomid and Pergonal, which prompt eggs to mature, are tested as infertility treatments.

1970

America's first commercial sperm bank opens in Minnesota.

1973

U.S. researchers Paul Berg and Stanley Cohen perform the first successful gene splicing, opening the way for gene therapy and the possibility of "designer babies."

1978

Louise Brown, the world's first test-tube baby, is born in England.

1981

Elizabeth Jordan Carr, the first in vitro baby in the United States, is born.

1984

Danish scientist Steen Willadsen clones a sheep from embryo cells, creating the first verified mammal cloning using the process of nuclear transfer.

1985

Congress, responding to complaints about unscrupulous fertility clinics, opens hearings into the practices surrounding IVF.

1990

Preimplantation genetic diagnosis, or PGD, is introduced as an experimental procedure. It involves removing a single cell from an embryo and testing it for genetic defects.

1992

Congress passes the IVF Success Rate Certification Act of 1992. It requires quality assurance and a disclosure of IVF success rates in all IVF programs. Scientists in Belgium develop a new IVF technique called intracytoplasmic sperm injection that revolutionizes the treatment of male infertility. A sixty-two-year-old Italian woman gives birth to a son after an IVF treatment.

1996

Dolly the sheep, the world's first mammal cloned from an adult cell, is born at the Roslin Institute in Scotland. The first child born as a result of MicroSort sperm-sorting technology is born.

1997

An Atlanta infertility clinic announces the first successful human pregnancy in the United States using an egg that had been frozen. The Society for Assisted Reproductive Technology is established at a meeting of the American Fertility Society. The McCaughey septuplets are born in Des Moines, Iowa, after their mother is treated with fertility drugs. They become the world's first surviving set of septuplets.

1998

Nineteen European nations sign a ban on human reproductive cloning. The U.S. Food and Drug Administration moves to regulate human cloning in the United States.

2001

Michael West and other scientists at Advanced Cell Technology in Massachusetts clone human embryos for the first time. Intended only for research, the embryos are not implanted.

2005

In a breakthrough with one of the most difficult mammalian reproductive systems, South Korean scientists clone a dog. They name it "Snuppy."

For Further Research

Books

Robin Baker, *Sex in the Future: The Reproductive Revolution and How It Will Change Us.* New York: Arcade, 2000.

Christopher L.R. Barratt and Timothy D. Glover, *Male Fertility and Infertility.* Cambridge, UK: Cambridge University Press, 1999.

Gay Becker, *The Elusive Embryo: How Women and Men Approach New Reproductive Technologies.* Berkeley: University of California Press, 2000.

Susan Cooper and Ellen Glazer, *Choosing Assisted Reproduction: Social, Emotional, and Ethical Considerations.* Indianapolis: Perspectives Press, 1998.

Dena S. Davis, *Genetic Dilemmas: Reproductive Technology, Parental Choices, and Children's Futures.* New York: Routledge, 2001.

Donna J. Haraway, *Simians, Cyborgs, and Women: The Reinvention of Nature.* New York: Routledge, 1991.

John Harris and Soren Holm, eds., *The Future of Human Reproduction: Ethics, Choice, and Regulation.* New York: Oxford University Press, 2000.

Alexina McWhinnie, *Families Following Assisted Conception: What Do We Tell Our Child?* Dundee, Scotland: University of Dundee, 1996.

Rozanne Nathalie, *Our Beautiful Work of A.R.T.* Minneapolis: Beaver's Pond Press, 2002.

Marlo M. Schalesky, *Empty Womb, Aching Heart: Hope and Help for Those Struggling with Infertility.* Minneapolis: Bethany House, 2001.

Judith S. Turiel, *Beyond Second Opinions: Rethinking Questions About Fertility.* Berkeley: University of California Press, 1998.

Carol Frost Vercollone, Heidi Moss, and Robert Moss, *Helping the Stork: The Choices and Challenges of Donor Insemination.* New York: John Wiley & Sons, 1997.

Periodicals

American Society for Reproductive Medicine, Society for Assisted Reproductive Technology, "Assisted Reproductive Technology in the United States: 1997 Results Generated from the Registry," *Fertility and Sterility,* October 2000.

Lori Andrews, "Reproductive Technology Comes of Age," *Whittier Law Review,* 1999.

Jason Barritt et al., "Cytoplasmic Transfer in Assisted Reproduction," *Human Reproduction Update,* July/August 2001.

B.D. Bavister and J.M. Squirrell, "Mitochondrial Distribution and Function in Oocytes and Early Embryos," *Human Reproduction,* July 2000.

Keith Betteridge, "Enigmas and Variations Among Mammalian Embryos," *Reproduction of Domestic Animals,* February 2001.

M.L. Boerjan, J.H. den Daas, and S.J. Dieleman, "Embryonic Origins of Health: Long-Term Effects of IVF in Humans and Livestock," *Theriogenology,* January 15, 2000.

Dan W. Brock, "Ethical Obligations to Prevent Genetically Transmitted Harms," www.utdt.edu.

Alexander M. Capron and Renie Schapiro, "Remember Asilomar? Reexamining Science's Ethical and Social Responsibility," *Perspectives in Biological Medicine,* Spring 2001.

Council of Europe, "Protocol Banning Human Cloning Enters into Force," *Council of Europe Press Service*, March 1, 2001. http://press.coe.int.

John Dawson, "Infertility Treatment: Posthumous Use of Sperm and Withdrawal of Consent: *Mrs. U v. Centre for Reproductive Medicine,*" *Medical Law Review,* October 2002.

Robert G. Edwards, "Ethical and Moral Issues of In Vitro Fertilization. Introduction: The Scientific Basis of Ethics," *Annals of the New York Academy of Sciences,* 1985.

B.J. Erb, "Deconstructing the Human Egg: The FDA's Regulation of Scientifically Created Babies," *Roger Williams University Law Review,* Fall 1999.

Karla Gale, "Assisted Reproduction 'Reasonable' Until Age 44," *Reuters Health,* August 22, 2005. http://today.reuters.co.uk.

Adam Greene, "The World After Dolly: International Regulation of Human Cloning," *George Washington Journal of International Law and Economics,* 2001.

J.C. Harper and J.D. Delhanty, "Preimplantation Genetic Diagnosis," *Current Opinion in Obstetrics and Gynecology,* April 2000.

Constance Holden, "Sperm-Free Fertilization," *Science,* July 20, 2001.

Steve Johnson, "Cloning Prospects Multiplying: Boom in Animal Products Possible from Advances," *San Jose Mercury News,* August 23, 2005.

Lori P. Knowles, "Reprogenetics: A Chance for Meaningful Regulation," *Hastings Center Report,* May/June 2002.

———, "Science Policy and the Law: Reproductive and Therapeutic Cloning," *Journal of Legislation and Public Policy,* Fall 2000.

Gina Kolata, "In Vitro Fertilization: Is It Safe and Repeatable?" *Science,* August 25, 1978.

H.J. Leese, I. Donnay, and J.G. Thompson, "Human Assisted Conception: A Cautionary Tale. Lessons from Domestic Animals," *Human Reproduction,* December 1998.

Alexina McWhinnie, "Euphoria or Despair? Coping with Multiple Births from ART. What Patients Don't Tell the Clinics," *Human Fertility,* February 2000.

Emily Nash, "First UK Designer Baby Joy," *Daily Mirror,* August 5, 2005.

Shaun D. Pattinson, "Reproductive Cloning: Can Cloning Harm the Clone?" *Medical Law Review,* October 2002.

———, "Wrongful Life Actions as a Means of Regulating Use of Genetic and Reproductive Technologies," *Health Law Journal,* 1999.

G. Petrelli and A. Mantovani, "Environmental Risk Factors and Male Fertility and Reproduction," *Contraception,* 2002.

John A. Robertson, "Reproductive Liberty and the Right to Clone Human Beings," *Annals of the New York Academy of Sciences,* September 2000.

Lee M. Silver, "Popular Cloning Versus Scientific Cloning in Ethical Debates," *Journal of Legislation and Public Policy,* Fall 2000.

Christine Stolba, "Overcoming Motherhood: Pushing the Limits of Reproductive Choice," *Policy Review,* January 2003.

D.A. Valone, "The Changing Moral Landscape of Human Reproduction: Two Moments in the History of In Vitro Fertilization," *Mount Sinai Journal of Medicine,* May 1998.

Web Sites

American Fertility Association (www.theafa.org). This is the Web site of a nonprofit organization that educates about fertility issues and advocates for support for infertile people. The site includes descriptions of issues and referral lists.

American Society for Reproductive Medicine (ASRM) (www.asrm.org). ASRM is a multidisciplinary organization for the advancement of the art, science, and practice of reproductive medicine. Its site includes news, reviews, and links.

Centers for Disease Control and Prevention (www.cdc.gov). Extensive information from the federal government's disease prevention agency can be found on this site. The site includes statistics on success rates and consumer advice.

Food and Drug Administration (www.fda.gov). This is the Web site of the federal regulatory agency that has primary jurisdiction over cloning activities.

Human Genome Project Information (www.ornl.gov). This Web site presents a lengthy fact sheet on human cloning, with additional links provided.

Infertility Resources for Consumers (www.ihr.com). Categorized links gathered by Internet Health Resources can be found on this Web site.

International Council on Infertility Information Dissemination (www.inciid.org). This is the Web site of a nonprofit organization dedicated to the exchange of information between fertility experts and those who suffer from infertility. The site includes forums for members and information on the group's programs.

IVF Connections (www.ivfconnections.com). This is a user-run forum and information site for consumers interested in in vitro fertilization.

National Conference of State Legislatures (www.ncsl.org). This Web site includes a useful survey of state laws on assisted reproduction as well as background information on relevant issues.

Organization of Parents Through Surrogacy (www.opts.com). The Organization of Parents Through Surrogacy is a not-for-profit, all-volunteer educational, networking, and referral organization that supports infertile couples in building families through surrogate parenting and other assisted reproductive technologies. Its site includes surrogacy resources, legislative alerts, and user forums.

RESOLVE: The National Infertility Association (www.resolve.org). RESOLVE is a nonprofit organization network of chapters mandated to promote reproductive health and to ensure equal access to all options for people experiencing infertility or other reproductive disorders. The site includes chapter listings.

Index

Crespi, Mary, 69–70, 73, 76, 77
Crespi, Steven, 69–70, 76
custody battles, 114–18

Daniels, Cynthia R., 35
Daniluk, Judith C., 128
Darlington, Lyell, 57, 58
den Boer, Andrea M., 223, 224, 226–28, 230
Desaulniers, Suzanne, 154, 155
Dietzen, John, 181, 182
Dolly (cloned sheep), 20, 106, 193, 200
Domar, Alice, 76
Donald, Ian, 60
Doniger, Wendy, 203
Donum Vitae (1987 papal encyclical), 178
Down syndrome, 54–55
    prenatal diagnosis of, 59–60
Doyle, Brian, 179

Edwards, Robert, 14, 61, 72, 80
eggs, 73, 170
    donation of, 81–82, 129
    extraction of, 63–64
Eichler, Margrit, 158
Ember, Melvin, 228
embryo(s), 16, 20, 82, 171
    personhood of, 17–18, 168–70, 176–78
    poor quality, detection of, 83–84
    splitting of, 109, 177
eugenics, artificial insemination and, 42, 44, 51–53
Eugenics Review (journal), 44
European Society of Human Reproduction, 21

Families in Canada Today: Recent Changes and Their Policy Consequences (Eichler), 158
Family Bonds: Adoption and the Politics of Parenting (Bartholet), 236, 241
family planning, 79
Feldschuh, Joseph, 48
Feminist International Network of Resistance to Reproductive and Genetic Engineering (FINRRAGE), 19
Fenwick, Lynda Beck, 159
Fertility and Sterility (journal), 47
Food and Drug Administration (FDA), 88
Foote, R.H., 25, 31
Fugger, Ed, 89, 91, 93, 94

Galton, Francis, 56–57
Gauthier, Marthe, 54
genetic engineering, 100–103
genetics, 55–58
Genetics & IVF Institute, 87
Gillon, Raanan, 198
Glenn, David, 221
Glossop, Robert, 157
Golden, Janet, 35
Goldstein, Joshua S., 227–28, 229, 231
Goldworth, Amnon, 17
Gosden, Roger, 78
Graham, Robert Clark, 47
Grogan, David, 142
Gylling-Holm, Jacob, 28

Haack, Susan, 177
Hall, Amy Laura, 172–73
Halliburton, Kim, 144, 149
Heape, Walter, 27
Henig, Robin Marantz, 72
Herman, Edward, 216
Hertwig, Oscar, 58